Beginning
Drama
11–14

Jonothan Neelands

David Fulton Publishers

London

David Fulton Publishers Ltd
Ormond House, 26–27 Boswell Street, London WC1N 3JD

First published in Great Britain by David Fulton Publishers 1998

British Library Cataloguing in Publication Data
A catalogue record for this book is available from the British Library

ISBN 1–85346–528–3

Typeset by FSH Print & Production Ltd, London
Printed in Great Britain by The Cromwell Press Ltd, Trowbridge, Wilts.

Contents

Acknowledgements

This book is dedicated to *the usual suspects* – you know who you are and will recognise your influence throughout these pages. A special thanks to Gavin Bolton, David Booth, Warwick Dobson and Fred Inglis for their acts of solidarity during the thesis writing. Thanks to David Booth and Mike Fleming for suggesting this book. Thanks also to Judith Ackroyd and Jo Trowsdale for their critical reading of early drafts.

I hope that those friends, teachers and PGCE students who remain unnamed will realise how much I have needed their time and support in this as in every project.

Year 7 Green Children – The Real Story first appeared in *English Language and Literature*, Series 2, Issue 3 © Stanley Thornes (Publishers) Ltd

Year 8 The Identification first appeared as Drama Work with Poetry, in *English Language and Literature*, Series 1, Issue 3 © Stanley Thornes (Publishers) Ltd

The Identification by Roger McGough is reprinted by permission of the Peters, Fraser & Dunlop Group Ltd, on behalf of Roger McGough.

Preface

Welcome to drama!

This is the second book in a series which is designed for student-teachers, non-specialist teachers who have an interest in knowing more and specialist teachers of drama who might need refreshing! *In Beginning Drama: 4–11* Joe Winston and Miles Tandy considered the role of drama in the primary phases of education. They described the role of drama as a medium for learning in many subjects of the primary school curriculum and laid out the beginnings of a course of study of drama as a subject. In that first book, the audience is assumed to be classroom teachers with a general responsibility for the whole curriculum including drama. Now, in this second book, we build on the advice and model of drama offered in the first book and move forward to the first years of secondary schooling. The key difference is that now we are considering drama as a specialist subject in the school curriculum, taught by a specialist teacher.

Some readers may be surprised by the scope, detail and complexity of some sections in this book. It is, after all, a beginners' guide. In our view it is important to begin with the idea that drama is a specialist subject that has its own curriculum framework, skills, concepts and knowledge. That is what this book tries to do – to introduce you to the foundation of knowledge, skills and experiences which together constitute the specialist study and practice of drama. It is quite possible to teach drama in the middle years without some of the specialisms described in this book, but we assume that you want to do more than follow other people's recipes without knowing, for yourself, how drama works.

The emphasis on drama as a subject in this book means that it has tried to cover, and integrate where possible, all that a specialist teacher might be asked to know and do. It assumes for instance, that a specialist will provide three dimensions of drama in the school: as curriculum subject; as extra-curricular activity and as community performance. There is also an emphasis on the long-term planning of curriculum objectives, progression and continuity, and assessment across the middle years and in preparation for the advanced study of drama in later years.

The book is written as a practical guide, or subject handbook; there are no references or quotations from other sources or to the extensive body of research that contributes to the ideas expressed. It is written as a synthesis of the drama education theories and practices that have been developed over the last two decades. I have tried to represent the richness of a community of teachers, researchers and theorists working in many different countries and contexts. Many of these people are represented in the bibliographies in the *Resources section* which also contains annotated guides to specialist drama education texts and resources. The bibliography is intended to guide you once you have completed this book.

Can this be drama?

For those of you who are new to teaching, your first experiences of drama in schools may offer a few surprises. The forms of drama to be found in schools often look and feel very different from the theatre experiences we have out of school. (You might want to look through some of the lesson structures contained in the *Resources section* before reading on if you are unfamiliar with school drama.) Why should this be?

In the popular imagination theatre is often thought of as the performance of plays by professional or amateur actors to a paying audience. It is a picture of theatre that is based on an economic agreement between the producers and the audience. The producers rehearse and develop a theatre product to the best of their abilities and, when the time comes, they perform their work in exchange for the price of a ticket.

More often than not the product that is exchanged is based on the work of a playwright. There is an assumption in this model of theatre that the majority of us will see, rather than be in, such plays. Acting, producing theatre, is seen as something only a few can achieve. There is also the assumption that the audience in this literary theatre will be silent and attentive to the work of the actors – audience responses are private rather than publicly shared as they might be in more popular forms of entertainment. I refer to theatre that corresponds to this image as belonging to the **literary and private aesthetic tradition**. If this popular image of theatre is the dominant one in most Western societies it should be remembered that there are alternative models of community theatre and performance which may bring us closer to recognising drama-making in schools as theatre.

In local communities in our society and in many traditional societies, the arts still serve the important civic and community functions that ritual and art-making once provided for us all. In the golden ages of Athenian and Elizabethan drama, for instance, going to the theatre was an important and integral part of the public life of the citizen. The theatre still offers communities a public forum for debating, affirming and challenging culture and community ties. In this community model, the arts are seen as important means of representing and commenting on the cultural life and beliefs of the community; in turn the communal participation of the whole community in art-making strengthens their cultural bonds. Every member of the group is seen as a potential producer – a potential artist. In this model, theatre is produced on the basis of a social agreement between members of a group who come together to make something that will be of importance to them: something that will signify their lives.

Drama that is produced on the basis of a social contract is likely to be local in its effect – its 'meanings' belong to the group who produces them and are addressed to the group as a whole. Because the live experience of communal performance is most important, such performances tend not to be recorded as play scripts – they are orally created and remembered. For this reason, communal drama belongs to what I will call the **oral and communal aesthetic tradition** which stresses the processes of production and the quality for participants of the immediate shared experience. The oral and communal tradition of non-literary and participatory entertainment is familiar to students from their experience of popular sports and entertainments and from their own community experiences of communal dancing, singing, storytelling and rituals.

This alternative social and community model of theatre shares some of the characteristics of drama in schools. A school is a community and drama is a living practice within it. The drama that young people make is often based on the concerns, needs and aspirations shared within the school community, or the community of a particular teaching group. It is often based on a social agreement that all who are present are potential producers – everyone can have a go at being actors and/or audience as the drama progresses. The coming together to make drama is also often seen as an important means of making the teaching group more conscious of themselves as a living community.

The forms that drama takes in school may also appear strangely different. There may be bewildering references to *tableau, hot-seating, thought-tracking*. This difference is partly due to the emphasis on joining in and making drama, so that many of these terms refer to ways in which drama can be made rather than watched. It is also due to a more pragmatic cause. Drama is taught in short periods of time, awkward spaces, to large numbers of students who are not all committed to doing it! These are not the conditions in which professional theatre is made. Drama teachers have developed ways of working and conventions that provide students with theatre experiences within these constraints. This book hopes to establish the theatrical foundations of this school-based version of drama and to show how it can lead to the study of theatre in other forms and contexts. This is the wonder of theatre, that a rich and multi-faceted variety of forms, conventions, genres and traditions have been spawned in response to the different needs and cultures of the contexts where it is produced.

ENJOY!

Ages and stages

This book covers the drama curriculum for students aged between 11 and 14. The references to Key Stages (KS) and Years reflect the English education system. The following guide is for readers who may be unfamiliar with this system.

Key Stage	Year	Age
KS1	1	5–6
	2	6–7
	3	7–8
KS2	4	8–9
	5	9–10
	6	10–11
KS3	7	11–12
	8	12–13
	9	13–14
KS4 (GCSE)	10	14–15
	11	15–16
POST-16	12	16–17
	13	17–18

The drama curriculum

How do we begin to plan a drama curriculum for the middle years? In this chapter we will consider the issues and elements of such a curriculum. This will include some discussion about what should be included and excluded, leading to a definition of theatre and the framing of aims and objectives. Further sections give advice on the principles of progression and continuity which might underpin the drama curriculum and suggest a framework for assessing students' achievements in drama.

The chapter closes with notes on the important relationship between drama and language development and a reminder of the vital role that drama can play in young people's lives and in the life of the school.

The field of drama

What should a drama curriculum cover? What are its priorities in the middle years of schooling? What will students be expected to know, understand and be able to do?

In our world the term 'drama' is used to refer to a diverse range of cultural practices which range from dramatic literature through to dramatic events in the news. In between we find the drama of TV and film, live theatre and the lived dramas of our personal and social lives. In our 'dramatised society' what is to be selected from the field of drama for inclusion and exclusion in a curriculum for drama?

The problem of making a selection from all the possibles in the contemporary field of drama is compounded by the problem of making a selection from the past. Whose histories and traditions do we include? There are obvious problems, in our pluralist and multicultural classrooms, in limiting the history of drama to those writers and practitioners who have contributed to the development of our modern Western theatre. The Western conventional theatre of the last hundred years or so has developed as a literary art, increasingly restricted to particular social groups and increasingly differentiated from other genres of popular drama and entertainment. Its selective tradition is often told in a form that suggests that the conventional theatre of our time is the natural evolution from earlier and inferior sources, particularly from the oral and communal traditions of performance. What messages does this send to students from cultures that have living performance traditions that are different? What does it tell students whose social and cultural history is different from the middle-class theatre audience?

What it is that we are preparing students to do in drama? In English, students become literate and effective speakers, listeners, readers and writers. In music and dance we prepare students to be players, dancers and critical audiences, but in drama there is an even wider range of roles that we might prepare students for: playwrights, dramaturges, actors, designers, technicians, directors, stage managers. Drama is the most social of all art forms; it uses a range of diverse skills and roles in its production. The range of roles is further extended when film and TV production are included in the drama curriculum.

Beyond these roles, there are also the roles and skills associated with the students' own use of drama both in the classroom and in school performances and extra-curricular drama clubs. The participatory and cooperative forms of theatre that have become associated with the practice of drama in schools require students to be effective negotiators, group members, researchers and devisers in addition to the conventional roles described above.

How can a drama curriculum cover so much?

Traditionally, approaches to curriculum planning in drama have tended to distinguish between 'theatre' and 'drama' In this distinction, 'theatre' is often taken to mean the study of the literature and practices of those conventional forms of professional and amateur theatre which have become associated with middle-class Western audiences (the literary and private aesthetic tradition). When this conception of 'theatre' operates, the emphasis is often on the formal study of the achievements of playwrights and on the skills needed to understand and appreciate their work in performance.

'Drama' on the other hand is taken to mean the practice of improvised and participatory forms of drama, which often derive their essentially oral and communal aesthetic from popular forms of entertainment. The practice of 'drama' is often seen as serving important and immediate personal and social purposes in young people's lives.

The problem with this historical distinction in drama education is that it drives an unnecessary wedge between two living traditions, or genres, of performance which ought to be studied and practised in harmony. Theatre can be both the literary professional theatre and the popular oral and communal theatre. It is part of the wonder of the art that it has developed so many different forms in response to the living contexts in which it is made and responded to. Theatre is one aspect of the cultural field of drama, but theatre is also a field in which there are many different positions, traditions, genres and histories.

There will always be problems with a drama curriculum that creates an imbalance between these exclusive concepts of 'theatre' and 'drama' and the aesthetic traditions that they represent. An emphasis on a socially restricted concept of 'theatre' may ignore many students' own experiences and everyday knowledge of drama and other forms of popular entertainment and may ignore the important contribution that drama education can make to students' own living experiences of the worlds in which they live.

To ignore the literary theatre tradition also results in exclusion. Knowledge and understanding of how such theatre is produced and how it is understood and fully appreciated is not generally available to all social and cultural groups. It has been historically restricted to those of a certain education and upbringing. For many students, school is the place where they too can be introduced to and enjoy the pleasures of the literary theatre while becoming conscious of its particular social history.

We need the kind of balance that many English teachers struggle for between reading and appreciating novels and the literary heritage, for instance, and encouraging students to use their own familiar linguistic and literary resources to communicate and interpret their own experience. It is a balance between acquiring the specific education required to decode and critically appreciate the literature and performance of theatre in the Western tradition and practising forms of drama which, like the mass-entertainment drama of film and TV, depend on knowledge and experience that is generally available for their enjoyment.

These problems of selection, inclusion and exclusion suggest an approach to curriculum planning in drama that focuses on the core skills and concepts that underpin the diversity of genres, histories and roles within the field of drama. A general foundation course will either prepare students for further vocational study in drama or provide them with the skills and knowledge to appreciate the role that drama will continue to play in their lives.

It is not just a question of balance in the curriculum between 'high' and 'low' dramatic practices, but of connection. Rather than reinforcing the socially-constructed differences between 'high' and 'low' forms of drama, a new conception of the dramatic curriculum should stress the connections: *the shared processes of production and reception.* There is no reason why dramatic literacy, like verbal literacy, cannot be taught through the vernacular and informal 'texts' and text-making processes that are familiar to, and representative of, the students themselves. This is the aim of the structures provided in the *Resources Section* – to teach the full range of dramatic literacy through making dramas that are inclusive of, and responsive to, the lives and maturity levels of 11–14-year-old students.

There is one further assumption to be made visible. I want to suggest that a drama curriculum should focus on the live experience of making and responding to theatre and that within this focus the emphasis should be on theatre as a **performance art** rather than on theatre as a branch of literature. In English-speaking countries, students will tend to encounter dramatic literature and to develop the codes of interpreting and responding to dramatic literature in English studies or language arts programmes. In many schools knowledge and understanding of the drama of film and TV may be taught as part of English or as Media Studies. It makes sense, therefore, to concentrate on how theatre is brought to life.

At first sight this assumption – that the drama curriculum should focus on live theatre – appears to be in contradiction to my earlier warnings about the ethnocentricity and social exclusiveness of the Western theatre tradition. What I am suggesting is that the drama curriculum should start from a definition of theatre that is inclusive of a wide range of theatre/drama practices and cultural traditions. A definition that rejects the hierarchisation of these practices into 'high/low', superior/inferior.

I have tried to draw out, from the potential field, certain characteristics that seem to be common to all forms of live theatre and to use these characteristics to offer a definition of theatre that is inclusive but also limited, in order to make some distinction between what is theatre and what is not theatre.

The four conditions of theatre

These conditions are:

| **1 An elected context** | Theatre is by choice. It is bracketed off from 'daily life'. It is a mode of *live* experience that is special and different from our everyday experience. The 'choice' is often formalised by the spatial and temporal separation of theatre from life, so that performances are advertised to occur at a certain time within a designated performance space. |

2 Transformation of self, time and place	Within the 'elected context' there is the expectation that a 'virtual present' or 'imagined world', which is representative of an 'absent' or 'other' reality will be enacted through the symbolic transformation of presence, time and space. The performance space, the experience of time and the actors all become something different for the duration of the performance.
3 Social and aesthetic rules/frame	Theatre is a rule-bound activity. Certain rules are 'perpetual' – there must be a choice as to whether an event is experienced as theatre, for instance. Others are tied to particular paradigms – the rules and conventions of a particular form or period of theatre. These rules relate both to the art of theatre and also to the terms of the social encounter that is theatre; being silent or joining in, for instance.
4 Actor–audience interactions:	There is always a performer function (the transformed self) and an audience function (reacting and responding to the performer's actions). In some forms of theatre these functions are clearly separated – the audience comes to communicate with actors. In others, the separation is less defined – a group come together to communicate as actors and as audience. Whatever form theatre takes, there must be communication between performer and audience.

Because of these four conditions, theatre is the live experience that is shared when people imagine and interact as if they were other than themselves in some other place at another time. Meanings in theatre are created by the actor, for both spectators and other participants, through the fictional and symbolic uses of human presence in time and space. These may be enhanced by the symbolic use of objects, sounds and lights. Theatre is understood through its conventions which are the indicators of the ways in which time, space and presence can interact and be imaginatively shaped to communicate different kinds of meanings.

Local vs National Curriculum

This discussion about the content and parameters of a curriculum for drama is only possible because, at the time of writing, drama is not a formal or National Curriculum subject in many countries. There isn't an agreed and legislative framework for drama as there is for Science or History. If such a framework existed then our discussion might be more concerned with its implementation and methods of delivery within a school. This situation is both a strength and a weakness.

The strength is that, in the absence of a national agreement about a drama curriculum, schools are free to design a curriculum for drama that is particularly responsive to local needs: to the local context for drama provided by a particular school representing a particular community. The local differences between what different communities might value in drama may be considerable. Here are three actuals from schools within a five-mile radius of each other:

Drama as personal and social education

In this school many of the students have low self-esteem and lack effective social skills for productive and constructive interpersonal relationships. Drama is not offered as an examination subject because the levels of truancy make it near impossible to complete the required practical coursework. In this school, drama is valued for the contribution it makes to the personal, social and moral education of the students as well as for being an immediate and practical forum for creativity. Drama is seen as being essential to the school's efforts to raise the expectations of both the students and the community and to develop the interpretative and interpersonal skills needed for the management of a happy and successful life. Understandably, the drama curriculum closely reflects the value and expectation that is placed on it by the school and its community. Its aims and objectives foreground the development and assessment of skills and objectives associated with the Personal, Social and Moral Education (PSME) curriculum.

Drama as English

In the second school, drama at KS3 (11–14) is taught as part of English but it has its own curriculum documentation and status. There are two strands that are emphasised – the personal and social rewards to be gained from the literary study, performance and watching of plays and the contribution that drama can make to the development of literacy. The aims and the objectives for the drama curriculum closely reflect the references to drama in the Statutory Orders for English and the assessment is either related to the national SATs for *Shakespeare* and *Speaking and Listening* or to written work in response to drama.

Drama as subject

The final school in the sample shares many of the social characteristics of the first but it is further into the process of regeneration. In a climate of league tables, performance indicators and local competition for resources the school is keen to boost the numbers of students achieving A–C grades in GCSE exams. In recent years drama students have done very well in their exams, and the school supports an increase in the number of students choosing drama as an exam option. Drama is taught by specialist teachers and the curriculum at KS3 is seen as a preparation for the GCSE course. There is a strong emphasis on the development and assessment of individual dramatic skills; the history of theatre, particularly Greek and Elizabethan; the production and presentation of plays by students. The aims and objectives for the KS3 curriculum are borrowed from the GCSE syllabus.

The different positions that have been taken in these schools goes beyond pragmatism and survival. They are not cynical responses to feeling marginalised. In all three schools drama is highly valued – but for different reasons. They are all positive attempts to frame a local interpretation of a drama curriculum.

Which brings us to the weakness of the local curriculum. There are two dangers. The first is professional insecurity. In the absence of a nationally agreed framework for drama, an individual drama teacher has no external and objective point of reference for her own curriculum plans. Am I doing the right things? Am I making fair assessments? What are other schools doing? The third school in our sample had used the aims and objectives from their GCSE syllabus for their KS3 curriculum, which is one way of tempering the local with an external validating authority. The second danger is that the local curriculum can be based on a highly idiosyncratic and ideologically motivated selection. What is taught may be left to the whim of an individual teacher and may reflect personal prejudices and interests rather than the breadth and depth of study which is a student's entitlement.

The potential strength of a curriculum that is based on a nationally agreed framework is that it provides a very visible and discussible curriculum. It is a public framework which gives students and their communities as well as schools a sense of what is expected, what is included and what will be assessed *in every school*. Different communities will respond to the content and ideology of national curriculum planning in different ways but at least a national agreement provides some external, relatively objective and visible material to discuss.

A common subject core: modes of activity

In England, where drama does not enjoy subject status within the National Curriculum, there are a number of national documents of guidance available as well as the specific references to drama in the Programmes of Study for English. In Scotland there are guidelines for drama within the national framework for Expressive Arts.

A close examination of the various sources of national guidance for drama reveals that there is some measure of general agreement that the aims and objectives for drama should reflect the three positions outlined earlier:

- Drama as personal, social and moral education
- Drama as English
- Drama as a subject in its own right.

There is also general agreement that drama, like the other arts, involves three interrelated modes of activity.

Making

This includes all the processes and stages of production used in the creation of a drama event whether it is a *tableau* or a full-length presentation. Making implies 'doing' but it also depends on 'knowing'. In other words, the student's 'making' is dependent on knowing *how* to make. In this sense, the assessment of students' making skills is in part an assessment of how well they have used what they have learnt about the processes of production in drama. Because drama is a social event the processes of production include the social and the aesthetic: the *social ability* to form effective production groups and to negotiate a dramatic representation that is itself representative of the production group; and the *aesthetic ability* to shape the representation into an appropriate form to communicate the production group's intentions.

The skills and understandings of making, or devising, drama that students need to develop might include:

- how to establish objective working relationships with other students regardless of gender, ability or personal prejudices;
- how to research, collate and select information needed for the work;
- how to translate a source for drama from page-to-stage: the source might be a playscript, story, poem, documentary text, image or idea;
- how to select and use an appropriate dramatic convention or form for the work;

- how to turn ideas about actions into actions;
- how to help to edit and refine a group's initial attempts at finding actions so that the performed action will stand alone without the need for further explanation or justification from the production group.

Performing

This includes the skills and knowledge needed for the execution of a drama event. Performance implies that there will be a transformation of self, time and space. A virtual 'reality', or 'drama world' will be communicated within the actual context of the classroom, studio or theatre. In the Western tradition of theatre the assumption is that a performance will be produced for another audience; there tends to be a rigid separation between the producers of the event and those who come to experience it. But performance can also mean a drama event that is shared among a group who may take it in turns to perform for each other or who may all be simultaneously involved in the performance of a virtual 'reality'.

The skills and understandings of performing that students need to develop might include:

- How can our daily behaviour and physical presence be transformed into 'other' characters, lives, physical presences?
- How do we choose a performance style: realism, symbolism, expressionism?
- How do we communicate different levels of meaning/interpretation through performance?
- How do we work effectively in ensemble performance: acting and reacting, giving and responding to cues?
- How can an actor's work be enhanced by light, sound and objects?
- How can spaces be transformed into 'other places' at 'other times'?

Responding

This includes the skills and knowledge of responding to drama in its written and performed forms. Responding includes articulating subjective responses to drama; making sense of feelings and thoughts aroused by the drama. It also includes the ability to deconstruct the drama using appropriate semiotic and critical codes; explaining how the elements of drama have been used to construct an effective dramatic instance. This process of critical deconstruction requires some objective knowledge of the 'grammar' of theatre and drama and of the histories of such 'grammars'. The skills and understandings of responding to theatre that students need to develop might include:

- How do we read dramatic literature as a potential performance text?
- How do we 'physicalise' a character from the clues given in a literary source?
- How do we deconstruct a moment of drama in terms of the elements used and its place within a dramatic structure or process?
- How do we begin to develop a critical and common language for making our own subjective response to drama public?
- How do we create the climate for giving and receiving public feedback on performance?

The three modes of drama – *making, performing, responding* – provide a basis for balance in a school drama curriculum. All three are associated with learning in drama and it is a teacher's responsibility to ensure that students engage with drama through each of the three modes. The detailed curricular framework for the activities will, however, still reflect local variations.

A common subject core: aims and objectives

The approved examination syllabi for Drama at GCSE provide teachers at KS4 (14–16) with a planned and nationally agreed curriculum for drama. For this reason, and because all students at KS3 are, potentially, working towards the levels of achievement in drama expected at GCSE level, it makes sense to consider the aims and objectives for GCSE as a model for framing aims and objectives at KS3.

The current GCSE syllabi for Drama reveal a general agreement about the broad aims for teaching and learning in drama and theatre at KS4. There are often three common aims to be found which cover:

1. understanding and using a wide variety of dramatic forms and concepts;
2. being an effective group member in making, performing and responding to drama;
3. the appreciation and review of live theatre experiences and evaluation of one's own performance and that of others.

I have translated these three broad aims into sets of objectives for a KS3 curriculum. There is sense in this plan as the common aims of GCSE provide some measure of external validation for a local school's curriculum and it ensures that there is progression towards KS4. However, we should remember that the majority of students who take drama at KS3 are unlikely to choose it as a vocational option for further study in the examination years. The KS3 curriculum has to be for all students and it should provide a synoptic conclusion for students who will not experience drama in KS4.

SUBJECT AIMS	SUBJECT OBJECTIVES
1 To understand and use a wide variety of dramatic concepts, genres and techniques	1.1 Learning about the creative and symbolic use of the elements of drama – time, space, presence, light, sound and objects – from their own experience of drama and from watching drama
	1.2 Learning how to use and control the elements of drama, particularly the body in space
	1.3 Learning to recognise and name the conventions and techniques used in drama and something of their history, e.g. monologue, tableau, role-play
	1.4 Learning to identify and distinguish historical and current genres of drama, e.g. tragedy, comedy, mime, mask, physical, soap opera
	1.5 Learning to use a variety of processes to devise and perform drama, e.g. improvisation, workshops, rehearsal, scripting, storyboards, characterisation
2 To work and perform as an effective group member	2.1 Learning to negotiate with others in a group and to adapt and accommodate to other people's ideas
	2.2 Learning to work as part of an ensemble – acting and reacting to others
	2.3 Learning about the different contributions that actors, audiences, directors, writers, designers and technicians make to a dramatic event
	2.4 Learning how to direct the work of writers, actors and designers into a coherent dramatic statement

3 To watch and appreciate a wide range of live theatre experiences and to be able to critically evaluate one's own and other people's performances	3.1 Learning and using a critical vocabulary for discussing drama, e.g. gesture, symbol, tension, rhythm and pace, contrast
	3.2 Learning to identify and evaluate the different choices that can be made in drama that lead groups to make different interpretations/representations of the same material
	3.3 Learning how to write reviews of drama that accurately refer to what was seen, heard and experienced during the drama
	3.4 Learning to distinguish and comment on the relationship between role codes and performer codes in drama, i.e. role code refers to the character and their place in the fiction of the drama (King Lear's changing relationship with his daughters); performer code refers to the actor's interpretation and execution of the character (the expressive and interpretative contribution that the actor makes to the character – e.g. Olivier's Othello, or McKellan's Richard 111)

I am suggesting that these aims and objectives will provide the groundwork at KS3 for further study of drama post-14. But the curriculum also needs to be mindful of the students previous experiences in drama. In England, as in many other countries, KS3 – the middle years of learning – represents a transitional period between the learning styles and teaching methods associated with the primary, or elementary, years and the increasingly subject-focused and performance-related teaching and learning that characterises much post-14 education. In this sense the KS3 curriculum should continue from previous experience and progress towards the next stage

Progression and continuity

Introduction

What does it mean to 'get better' at doing drama? How should the drama curriculum be sequenced so that it ensures that there is progressive challenge for students? In this section, I want to discuss some of the problems and considerations of progression in drama and then to suggest some principles and activities that might help to provide a visible and coherent plan for progression in KS3.

Lack of continuity

The lack of a national framework for drama together with the patchy provision of drama in KS1/2 (5–11) makes it difficult for teachers in KS3 to know what prior experiences students might have had in drama. Some may have had regular classes in drama in school. Some may have received private classes in drama and dance. Some may (because of social and geographical circumstances) be regular theatregoers. We have noted that a curriculum for drama should not be based on the assumption that all children have had all or any of these prior experiences. However, it is safe to assume that the majority of children coming into KS3

- will have experienced some form of imaginative and imitative role play in school or in the community;
- will also be aware that people behave as social actors who take on roles that are appropriate to social situations;
- will watch, understand and regularly discuss drama on TV, video or film most nights of the week;
- will have some sense of narrative genres, structure and plot development, even if this is no more than a simple beginning, middle and end structure and an awareness that stories sequence people and events in time and space;
- will have some sense of *cultural logic*, in other words, their own socialisation will have taught them something about how people might behave and react in particular circumstances. Children's responses to the question: 'What happens next?' often reveal their sense of narrative (this is what usually happens in a story like this) and their sense of cultural logic – 'my existing understanding and observation of human behaviour makes me think that this would happen next'.

Diversity of purposes

As we have seen, drama serves a number of different functions in a school as subject, as English and as a form of community art-making. We have also noted that the priorities of the curriculum might differ from school to school. In some schools progression might be understood in terms of developing dramatic literacy, in others in terms of personal and social development and in others progression might be looked for in terms of developing language and literacy skills.

Levels of dramatic literacy

The field of drama encompasses both the drama of the large scale productions of TV and film and the restricted production of mainstream 'serious' theatre. There are differences in the modes of literacy demanded. Large-scale productions tend not to require any formal study or specific education from their audiences; they would not have the same commercial appeal if they did. However radical and complex they might at first seem, the new dramatic conventions and techniques that film and TV introduce are quickly recognised and absorbed as part of most students' everyday knowledge and experience.

The restricted art of theatre, however, is in part restricted because it does require formal study and a certain level of education from its audience; it is restricted to those who have the knowledge of theatre codes, conventions and histories. We know enough from our everyday experience of drama to understand and make sense of *EastEnders* or *Jurassic Park* but we are unlikely to make as much sense of *Waiting for Godot* or *The Ghost Sonata* without prior knowledge of the theatre traditions they belong to.

Most of the drama at KS3 is likely to draw on students' everyday knowledge of drama, but during KS3 students should, as the aims and objectives have suggested, begin to be introduced to the codes and histories of the conventional theatre. This should not be seen as, or treated as, a progression from one to the other. Rather it should be seen as a progression towards a more inclusive drama curriculum: in other words both traditions are approached horizontally rather than vertically.

For many KS3 students their first introduction to the restricted art of theatre is likely to be through Shakespeare. It may be the first time that students encounter drama that is 'difficult', in other words a drama that is not immediately understood or gratifying. In order to ease this transition many teachers work with a sense of progression, so that in KS3 the emphasis tends to be on plot, character and setting while in KS4 the same plays may be looked at in terms of language, metaphor and dramatic structure.

In the table opposite I have taken one aspect of the drama curriculum – making and responding to a dramatic action – and suggested what progression might mean in that one aspect. An 'action', it must be remembered, might be speech, gesture, movement or the placing of an object or design feature such as lighting.

Progression in dramatic action: making, performing and responding

Making/performing	Responding
1 Proposing 'next action' in a narrative sequence	Understanding relationship between 'next action' and the narrative sequence
2 Executing an action in the belief that it will provoke a reaction	Understanding the causal relationship between actions taken
3 Executing an action that is 'culturally' true to the 'given circumstances'	Recognising the action as being 'context specific'
4 Combining physical and inanimate actions – use of props, sounds, lights etc.	Recognising and commenting on the relationship between physical and inanimate actions
5 Executing actions at the level of 'gestus' or symbol rather than at the level of social/cultural sign	Recognising and commenting on the selectivity and resonance of actions
6 The *practised* execution of an action according to a given intention	Recognising and commenting on both the processes of rehearsal and the artistic/aesthetic quality of the execution of an action
7 Directing and executing a sequence of practised actions to create a sustained dramatic statement	Understanding and commenting on the 'dramaturgy' or weave of the actions that constitute a dramatic statement

Note: Levels 1–5 describe the potential stages of progression in KS3. Levels 6–7 require a highly specialised education which is only likely to be introduced at KS4 and beyond.

Role progression

A key consideration at KS3 will be the progression from simple role-taking to more complex forms of dramatic characterisation. At KS2, and during KS3, students' enjoyment of drama is often based on their active involvement and absorption in the fiction. Like a game, it is fun to take part and to experience the emotional twists and turns of the drama for one's own enjoyment. As students become more experienced and involved in making, performing and responding to drama they will want to learn how to 'act' – how to play someone who is different and in so doing how to communicate to an audience the emotional twists and turns of the drama. Students understand from their everyday experience that any social event involves role-taking of some sort.

When in public we consciously project a public image of self that is appropriate to the circumstances we find ourselves in. These public images may express a social role such as parent or teacher and they may project an image of self such as being hard, cool, or not interested in boys/girls! The aesthetic actor builds on this idea of the social actor to create a public role that is a projection of another identity – to behave as Macbeth.

In the next table, I have tried to identify the stages of role progression that take students from being social actors to being aesthetic actors. I am aware that the stages assume that the psycho-realist acting style associated with realism and the actor training system developed by Stanislavski represents the highest level of acting achievement. There are, of course, other traditions and uses of acting but for many young people the 'realism' of the Stanislavskian tradition is a measure of the quality of the acting they see on film and TV.

Role development	Requirements	Evidence
1 Public self in the social setting of the classroom	Self-consciousness and fear prevents students from being anything other that their 'usual self'. Whatever the circumstances the student behaves as they would in any social situation that involved their classmates	May not take any active part in the drama. May constantly refer to the 'real events' in the classroom when expected to be in role, e.g. 'I don't like her, I'm not working with her' or 'This is stupid, I don't know what to do, Miss'
2 Public self but operates as a role in the social setting of the drama	Takes a part in the drama and recognises the given circumstances of the fiction, but still responds as 'self' rather than imagining and communicating the responses of someone who is 'different'	Takes part in the working out of the dilemmas and situations to be faced in the drama but as if they were themselves facing these situations, i.e. this is how I would actually respond. Cannot recognise that others in the group might be projecting an imagined self that is 'different' from their usual selves

3 Operates as a role, but now projects a social or cultural attitude to events, which is different from normative or habitual self	Self-selects or is given a characteristic attitude to play in response to events and other characters. Student begins to imagine, and play with, how someone who is different might respond and behave in the circumstances of the drama	Student begins to think about, respond and project as a character who is 'different', i.e. how would this 'other' person respond to what is happening? The difference may be of gender, age, status, physicality, culture or class
4 Operates as above but role taken is representative of a social or cultural group with its own history and characteristic response	Researches, projects and plays as a role who is characteristically different and who has a clear sense of a past and a destiny	Considers and tries to incorporate in their playing, the effects of history and environment on the identity of a character. Plays a 'type' of person in the Brechtian sense
5 Uses technique to 'become' a character who is physically and psychologically unique	Creates and develops a detailed psychological profile, or sub-text, which reveals individual motives, ambiguities and paradoxes. Finds and develops appropriate gestures and actions to communicate this complexity to others	Tries to differentiate character from others of the same type, i.e. not just a villager, but a particular villager who has unique characteristics. Plays with the ambiguities, tensions and paradoxes of a particular human life
6 Projects self as actually being the character – the performer's 'self' is masked by her physical manifestation of a 'flesh-and-blood' character	Is able to communicate the 'truth' of a character. In other words the performer now appears, in performance, to actually be, and always have been, the character	Is able to 'transform' both physically and psychically into a highly detailed manifestation of character

Note: Levels 1–4 describe the potential stages of progression in KS3. Levels 5–6 require a highly specialised education which is only likely to be introduced at KS4 and beyond.

Three key principles of progression in drama

With our discussion of progression in mind, I want to suggest that there are three principles of progression in drama which might inform the drama curriculum at KS3. These principles are:

1.   Students should progressively take responsibility for making *informed* choices about the form and direction of their work

But the ability to make informed choices is dependent on and limited by:

- knowledge and experience of 'form' and the histories/traditions of 'form'; knowing what the 'choices' are;
- the skills needed to articulate and negotiate ideas with others in and out of the artistic process;
- knowledge and experience in matching 'means' and 'meanings'; recognising that form creates content, content suggests form.

You can't take responsibility unless you have been given responsibility!

2.   Students should become increasingly selective and complex in their use of 'sign' and gesture to make and represent meanings

But this ability is dependent on the degree of explicit attention that the curriculum has given to:

- *reflexiveness:* drawing attention to 'theatre-as-theatre' rather than as an 'illusionary experience'; the 'nuts-and-bolts' of theatre production – how the elements and conventions of drama are being used – are made visible to students;
- *dramaturgy:* drawing attention to the 'weave' of the actions in a drama event; students regularly analyse how moments of effective drama are constructed or choreographed;
- *modelling:* providing live experience and analysis of theatre artists working in a variety of forms and traditions.

3.   Students should be assessed on what they make rather than on what they claim, or are imagined, to experience

But in KS3 there should be an increasing emphasis on students being able to make drama as well as to experience teacher-led structures.

In the mainstream tradition, writings and other forms of commentary on theatre tend to focus on psychological questions in the work:

- how a performance reveals the private and social psychology of a character;
- how the actor must work on understanding and revealing the psychology of a character;
- how an audience is psychologically affected by a performance.

Despite this emphasis, we shouldn't base our assessments on what we imagine to be the private psychological states of the students – their 'belief' and 'depth of feeling' for example. What is assessable is either what we see and hear them do in their drama work or some account or analysis of their experience that can also be seen or heard by others.

Progression in theatre-making

In order to ensure that the principles of progression can operate in practice, the curriculum needs to provide an increasing challenge to the students' ability to make, perform and respond to drama. The curriculum can be seen as a form of 'scaffolding' which, through a carefully wrought frame of steps and stages, allows students to build on their existing and prior experiences and knowledge of drama towards the experience and knowledge that they will either need for further study or for a terminal point in their school-based drama experience.

In the following table I have suggested certain progressions that a drama curriculum might develop. The categories respond to a *pedagogic progression* from the simple unreflexive realism of younger students' drama making, in which the teacher is very much at the centre of a class's work, towards students being given and taking increasing responsibility for their own group work with the teacher working in the margins, guiding, managing, monitoring and assessing the work of groups.

The categories also reflect a certain *aesthetic progression*, or directions, in the development of twentieth century Western theatre. These directions are characteristic of the avant-garde line of Meyerhold, Brecht, Grotowski and Boal and other practitioners who pioneered different post-naturalist theatre movements – symbolism, expressionism, physical, and social expressionism – to challenge the dominance of realism and naturalism in the conventional theatre. Once again, it is important to stress that the progression is not hierarchical: it is historical. The forms of drama that younger students enjoy and the forms of theatre that they draw on will continue to play an important role in their drama work and leisure.

From (KS2)	Progression (KS3)	To (KS4)
rules	**from** simple structures based on rules of game, or taking turns, or pursuing simple objectives: arguing, persuading, describing events	
	towards language and behaviour determined by the frame, the given circumstances of the situation that is being dramatised. Structures that require students to communicate the relationship between text (actions) and context (situation)	**frame (given circumstances)**
social actor	**from** taking on and acting out the roles and responsibilities of the adult world. Role actions and reactions conform to social codes and courtesies, e.g. meetings. Status relationships. Taking direct action that will resolve or develop social problems and dilemmas	
	towards using the body expressively, i.e. with the intention of communicating character to others. Selective and conscious use of external actions and reactions to illustrate and comment on the inner life of characters; physically playing text and sub-text	**aesthetic actor**
direct mimesis	**from** the making of 'life-like' representations of people, places and events in which the apparent 'realism' of the representation is taken as a measure of its 'truthfulness' or authenticity – enactments of life in a Viking village or a Victorian poorhouse for instance	
	towards more subtle and reflexive forms of dramaturgy that focus on the interpretation of experience and the representation of themes – episodic; montage; use of elements of symbolism	**expressive interpretation**
sign	**from** recognising and using conventional, or stock, signs to convey mood, purpose or response, e.g. hanging head to express disappointment, clenching fists to express frustration or anger. These kinds of conventional sign mean the same whoever is signing	
	towards more subtle and resonant use of gesture; signs that are expressive of, and particular to, a ifferentiated character or situation, or theme in the drama	**symbol (gestus)**

	from	
type	making and taking roles based on cultural or occupational types or collective identities, e.g. villager, worker, parent, soldier. 'How would the villagers respond?'	
	towards	
	playing characters with particular social, historical, physical and psychological 'characteristics' that the student either creates or interprets. 'How would *this* villager respond?'	**character**

	from	
linear narrative	story drama structures based on a simple sequence of events acted out naturalistically. The focus is on cause-and-effect and narrative logic	
	towards	
	complex episodic structures where the sequence is organised thematically rather than temporally. The order of episodes is designed to deepen response to the 'meaning' of events or the 'sub-text' and may use symbolic and expressive conventions, e.g. alter-ego, dance, mask, tableau	**montage**

	from	
illusionary	the 'realism' of 'living through' imagined experiences as if they were actually occurring; where the emphasis is on creating a subjective 'authenticity' or 'reality'	
	towards	
	a greater emphasis on *how* drama is made and *what* it is made of. The 'illusion' of a virtual reality is broken and there is a greater emphasis on the shaping and presentation of work which shows the students' objective control and use of the elements of drama	**reflexive**

	from	
teacher-centred (whole group)	work that is initiated and led by the teacher who often works within the drama (as fellow actor, with the whole class responding in role) to model register and role; to create tension for the students; to challenge and support students	
	towards	
	work that is devised in small groups in response to 'tasks' set by the teacher or decided on by groups. Students are expected to make creative decisions about how best to execute the work	**autonomous dramaturges (small group)**

Assessment

How and by what means do we assess drama? Any assessment should provide a fair, reliable and objective means of placing a student's progress in drama. But there are pragmatic and philosophical issues to be resolved.

Pragmatic issues

The frequency, rigour and detail of assessment in drama will vary according to a number of local factors: some of which we have already discussed.

As we have already noted, at a local level schools value drama for different reasons and this valuing will reveal itself in the assessment arrangements. In some schools assessment may focus on the personal and interpersonal behaviour of students. In others the assessment of drama may be subsumed into the assessment of English: the contribution that drama makes to the development of linguistic and literary skills and knowledge. In schools that view KS3 drama as a foundation and recruiting ground for KS4, assessment might focus on student's preparedness for further studies in drama leading to a qualification. The demands for accountability in drama may also vary from school to school according to the value that drama is given in the curriculum: some schools may require and take note of detailed assessments in drama; in others there may be little point in providing any detail beyond an assessment of a student's level of confidence and willingness to work with others in an effective way.

The *time* given to drama will also be subject to local variations. Students who study drama in 35-minute lessons during KS3 cannot be expected to achieve the same standards, or depth and breadth of study, as students who have one-hour lessons. Teachers who are trying to provide meaningful experiences of drama in very short time periods may also be reluctant to spend precious time on the detailed individual assessment of pupils. Access to *resources* will also affect students' opportunity to develop their abilities to the standards set. In many schools, students have limited access to *all* the elements of drama. Use of space is, for instance, a key skill in all drama work; but it is difficult to develop this skill in the limited space of a classroom, cloakroom or cupboards that some teachers are forced to teach drama in. Similarly, the technical ability to use contrasts of light and sound will depend on access to technology in a school.

There are also considerable problems related to the *assessment of individuals* in what is an essentially social and ephemeral activity. The problems are of visibility and evidence of individual achievement. Drama teachers, particularly at KS3, tend to have a relationship with groups rather than individuals. In the English classroom, students are often engaged in private work even if it is done in social circumstances. The nature of teaching and learning in English allows the teacher to spend time in one-to-one contacts with students. Assessment tasks in English tend to be undertaken individually and provide a permanent archive of evidence of a student's development. Drama teachers, on the other hand

- see groups for shorter periods;
- set goals for groups, rather than individuals, to work on;
- work towards group or whole-class presentations that are not permanently recorded and
- if teaching drama to a whole year-group, find it very difficult to keep track of every student.

Philosophical issues

In addition to the practical problems of assessment, there are also philosophical issues that relate to the purposes of drama work and the assessment of 'creativity'.

Drama teachers are responsible for developing and balancing two different aesthetic traditions: the literary and private and the oral and communal.

In the literary and private aesthetic associated with the restricted art of theatre there are specific skills associated with the production and reception of theatre that will reveal individual strengths and weaknesses. We comment on the relative skills of different actors: for instance, we audition actors and select them on the basis of their individual skill-levels. At an amateur level, groups and individuals often take part in competitions or graded tests to establish levels of individual achievement. The ability to decode dramatic literature and to produce a written review of performances also requires individual skills that some students will possess to a greater extent than others.

In the oral and communal aesthetic, associated with popular forms of entertainment and community art-making, the emphasis tends to be on the quality of the social experience and what is produced collectively rather than on the quality of individual skills and contributions. In the oral and communal tradition individual differences are masked by the social effects of a group who pool their strengths in order to work towards communal goals. In a real sense, the willingness to take part, regardless of individual ability, is seen as being more important than demonstrating who is the most artistically skilled in the group. In this sense, much of the drama work that is done in KS3 will serve the same purposes as other communal art – community singing, dancing, storytelling, ritual. In these community circumstances we often tend to evaluate the live experience that we share and the communal pleasure of the event rather than the skills of those involved. If I go, as audience, to see a professional dance company, I expect my pleasure to come from the skills of the dancers. If I go clubbing, I want to have a good night out dancing with others – I don't want any feedback on my dance skills, or comment on my physical shape and grace!

In an assessment programme that focuses too strongly on differentiating between students on the basis of their individual abilities as performers and respondents in drama, there is a danger of alienating and disempowering students who have neither the restricted skills, nor the inclination to develop them, but who nonetheless derive enormous social and aesthetic benefits from participating in drama. In a programme that ignores the development and assessment of individual skills, those students who have a vocational interest in drama are denied the teaching and assessment they need to develop their individual performer skills. There is a further danger that, in some schools, the reluctance to make individual and visible assessments will be taken as a sign that drama is not a legitimate subject for academic study and reward.

In modern Western societies there is still a belief that 'artists' are specially inspired people who have exceptional 'natural' gifts and whose 'creativity' is also a rare and mysterious quality. This belief leads to a reluctance to make subjective assessments of the 'quality' of students' art work, or to subject their attempts at 'self-expression' to external judgement. Increasingly, however, we are becoming aware that artists are often specially trained rather than specially gifted and that this special training is often made more available to students from certain social groups. It is only in the last fifty years or so that we have seen professional actors who are neither middle class nor European in their origins (although actors often enjoyed the same social status as tinkers prior to the nineteenth century). We are also aware that we all 'create' and exchange our worlds through acts of perception and communication.

The arts are, in this sense, no more than and no less than specialised forms of communication which draw on many of the same skills required in any other form of communication – the ability to communicate experience, which is based on a particular perception of the world, to others in a way that allows them to share and respond to that experience as if it was their own. In this sense drama is a form of communication in which *meanings* are shared through the *means* of dramatic conventions.

Some students will communicate more effectively through drama than through other means, just as some students will demonstrate a particular aptitude for the sciences or for sport, but as with written forms of communication all students require training and instruction in how to use the formal means of communication in drama if they are to achieve their potential. And this training can be objectively assessed just as it is in written forms of communication.

Drama standards at KS3

Aims	Standards at KS3	Grade

Grade descriptions

1 Developed = Consistently demonstrates the standards. Makes independent use of skills and knowledge and can apply them in a variety of contexts.

2 Developing = Demonstrates most of the standards in some modes of drama. Needs support in order to achieve/demonstrate potential and to apply learning.

3 Emergent = Demonstrates levels of ability which are below KS3 standard. Needs considerable help and encouragement to achieve/demonstrate potential. Is not certain or confident about applying learning.

4 Challenged = Has made little progress. Needs constant supervision and support and is reluctant to demonstrate potential in drama.

Aims	Standards at KS3	Grade
1 Understands and can use a wide variety of dramatic concepts, genres and techniques	1.1 Makes creative and symbolic use of the elements of drama	————
	1.2 Knows how to use and control the elements of drama	————
	1.3 Can recognise and name the conventions and techniques used in drama	————
	1.4 Can identify and distinguish historical and current genres of drama	————
	1.5 Has used a variety of processes to devise and perform drama	————
2 Works and performs as an effective group member	2.1 Negotiates with others in a group and adapts to other people's ideas	————
	2.2 Works effectively as part of an ensemble	————
	2.3 Understands the different artistic contributions that make a drama	————
	2.4 Can direct the work of others into a coherent dramatic statement	————

3 Is able to critically evaluate own and other people's performances	3.1. Uses a critical vocabulary for discussing drama	———
	3.2. Can identify and evaluate the different artistic choices that can be made in drama	———
	3.3. Knows how to write reviews of drama	———
	3.4. Can distinguish and comment on the relationship between role codes and performer codes in drama	———

This table is intended to describe the potential field of assessment. It will, of course, need to be modified to take local factors and priorities into account. The grid is also related to the assessment of subject skills and knowledge – it doesn't include standards associated with the PSE or English curricula. For local reasons teachers may want to negotiate and include other aims and standards that go beyond the practice of drama as a subject.

The means of assessment

If assessment is to be used as the basis for establishing levels of ability and discussing development then it must be permanent, visible and discussible. There has to be some lasting record of achievement that can be referred to by teachers, students and parents. It must be visible in the sense that all parties can see, hear or read the same material rather than consider accounts of student practice that do not reveal the evidence that is used. It must create the possibility of dialogue about the fairness of the assessment and the negotiation of future goals and targets for improvement. The means of assessment must also be fit for the purpose. There is, as we have noted, a diverse range of skills and activities in drama which may require different instruments for their assessment.

This table describes some of the commonly used means of assessment in drama.

Instrument	Description
Journals and diaries	Notebooks or folders kept by students that contain a record of their responses and working processes during the drama. These may be informal and based on written student-teacher dialogues or structured so that specific tasks, e.g. a character description, are set.

Writing and scripting	Scripted dialogues and/or scenes that might be originals, interpretations or dramatisations from other sources including improvisation. Assessment is tied to the realisation of particular dramatic intentions or conventions. Writing that emerges from drama – letters, diaries, petitions, instructions, dispositions etc.
Video and sound records	Video or oral record of class work taken by the teacher or student that is a permanent record of a student's level of ability at a chosen moment
Written and standardised tests	Formal tests of students' knowledge of texts, genres, history. National standardised tests such as the Shakespeare and Speaking and Listening SATs at KS3
Art work	Permanent records of students' making and responding in the form of masks, collages, soundtracks, set or costume design, poetry or narrative
Seminar/demonstration	Students research, plan and then lead group discussion on some aspect of drama, e.g. their research into a character, issue or historical period. Students physically demonstrate and comment on an aspect of their drama-making, e.g. the different ways a role could be played, or how they made a mask
Self-evaluation profile	Students are regularly given a checklist of objectives for their work and offer a self assessment of their progress and cite their own evidence to support their assessment. These self-assessments are agreed/not agreed by the teacher in discussion

Drama and language development

So far, we have concentrated on the planned drama curriculum – a curriculum that is restricted to the formal study of selected concepts, practices, skills and experiences from the potential field of drama. In this section we are going to consider the interrelationship between drama and selected aspects of language and literacy development. We have noted that the positive benefits of using drama methods as part of the study of English and language arts is often an important consideration for schools. In many schools drama is taught under the umbrella of English, by teachers whose first specialism is English. For these reasons, the planned drama curriculum may include additional aims and objectives which are related to an explicit focus on literacy and language development as part of drama.

Dramatic literature

There is a long tradition in English-speaking countries of studying and experiencing drama as part of the study of English language and literature. Historically, this is a reflection of the 'literary-ness' of the English speaking theatre. In a theatrical tradition that gives greatest value to the work of playwrights it is inevitable that the study of dramatic literature should become part of English studies. It continues to be important to introduce students to historical and contemporary dramatic literature, both as drama and as literature. Such study gives students both the pleasure and challenge of a writer's work and also provides access to the performance codes and histories of the literary theatre. Understanding a writer's intention through close reading and then deconstructing it and physically reconstructing it as a performed text is an important learning process for students to follow.

Registers and codes of communication

Reading and performing extracts from dramatic literature represents an obvious relationship between English and drama, but in recent years this relationship has been extended in new directions. Increasingly, we have become aware of language as a socially constructed system. Our use of language is highly 'situational' and culturally determined. In other words, much of what we say and do is bound to the situations that we find ourselves in; different situations require different uses of language. It is through language that we make our private meanings public – communicable to others – and this making public depends on there being a shared set of linguistic resources among the communicating group. If I want to tell you what I'm thinking and feeling, I have to put it into a form of communication that we both understand and which is appropriate to the situation that we find ourselves in. If I have had a nasty car crash which has caused me distress, I might need to share this distress through communicating it to others. The form through which this communication takes place (and therefore the 'meaning' of distress that I communicate) will be different according to whether I am communicating with:

- the police at the scene of the accident
- staff at the hospital where I have been taken
- my family when I get home
- friends who phone to see if I'm all right
- my insurance agent who comes to inspect the damage
- the magistrates at a court hearing.

In addition to these possible 'speech events' there will also be the need to communicate through writing, and again each of the different events will require a different form of writing – the statement to the police, the report for the insurance cover, a letter to a friend. In a social theory of language – a theory that connects the way that we communicate with the social circumstances in which we communicate – the form of communication is referred to as *register*. There are three elements to register which when taken together provide a means of analysing communication events:

1. **Discourse:** What is the content that is being discussed? At first sight it might seem that in each of the examples I gave for the car crash, the discourse was the same. It was about my car crash. But, in fact, there may well be subtle differences of discourse. In talking to the police and the magistrates my discourse, or 'sub-text' in dramatic terminology, may actually be more to do with what an innocent victim I am rather than the details of the accident. In talking to my family, my discourse may be more to do with my need for a hug!
2. **Tenor:** What is the relationship that I am establishing with others? The examples range from establishing a formal, perhaps even deferential, relationship – with the police and magistrates for instance – through to the intimate relationship I wish to establish with family members.
3. **Mode:** What form, or genre, of communication is being used? We can make a basic distinction between talking and writing, but distinctions can also be made within these categories. Mode is the most culturally codified element of register. We have evolved certain conventions of communication which are 'appropriate' for certain kinds of events and not others. To be literate one must know of these coded forms, how to observe the conventions and when to use a particular form. As a literate member of my culture I understand that each of the examples that I have given will require different codified forms of communication:

- making a *statement* to the police
- giving *witness* in a court
- giving an *account* to the insurance company
- retelling the event as an *anecdote* for friends and family.

To be literate, in the sense that one can recognise, use and control register is to be socially powerful. It gives you control over the communication events that you encounter. This level of literacy and the power that it brings have traditionally been associated with the education and upbringing of particular social groups rather than others. In other words, some children are more likely to experience through family and schooling the nuances and variety of language registers in a culture than others. If you are brought up in a professional home where the family members possess a high level of literacy, you are more likely to have experienced a variety of registers of language use than if you are brought up in a family that has not traditionally been educated or experienced in using language in *different* situations for different purposes.

Because, as we have seen, drama is so 'situational' it provides a means of giving all students experience and knowledge of register. The examples of communication events related to the car crash can all be enacted and analysed in the classroom. The different modes of writing can all be incorporated into that drama. Through the construction and experience of different kinds of situation related to the same events, all students can experience the power of literacy.

In our lived experience we operate in various social roles, we choose and use different registers and adopt/switch dialects according to the experience of the situation we are in. This is also what happens in drama.

- *We imagine that we are in a different physical and social situation from that of the classroom.* In drama, language is only one of the forms used to represent the situation. We don't just talk ourselves into the context. We also make meaningful use of space, gesture and objects to define both the physical and the social elements of the situation.
- *We take on new roles.* What we say and do is determined by who we are in the drama and the demands of the situation that we face.
- *We interact with others.* We establish our social relationship with the other players through language and actions – the language we each use expresses our needs and intent in the drama but it also symbolises our position in the social structure and hierarchies of the drama. If my role is that of a lawyer, I choose my words to communicate information but I also choose them to show that I am lawyer – I will talk like a lawyer.
- *We learn new language from the experience.* The drama experience, like a life experience, becomes a personal resource which can help us grow in our knowledge and use of language.

Embodied language

We can talk about language in the abstract, but our lived experience of language is immediate and physical. One of the problems of cultural representation that drama solves is to provide a means of representation in the *present* tense. To show life as it is being lived rather than to report on events that have already been lived. Whatever form drama-making takes, the challenge is to 'embody' words and ideas. Taking a character from the page and turning it into a character on the stage means having to translate dialogue and stage directions into physical actions and reactions. The idea of Hamlet becomes a flesh-and-blood actual presence; we smell him and see his *physical* torment. In improvisation, when we are as uncertain of what others might say as we are in life, we are physically affected by what we say and what others say to us; we experience actual surprise, the sweat of tension, pain and sadness. In both forms of drama, we experience language but we also experience the 'experience' that language seeks to convey.

Deconstruction

In the processes of rehearsal, actors use the elements of drama – the conventions of time, space and presence – to deconstruct the texts they are working on, so that they can eventually be reconstructed as a performance text. The purpose of rehearsal and workshops is to explore meanings, characters and ideas and try out possible interpretations. Rather than discussing interpretation, actors use drama – use role and space and time – to reveal the nuances of text. In the same way, students can use the conventions of drama as a means of exploring and discovering what lies beneath the surface of the texts they engage with in the English classroom. They can:

- enact scenes in the original text;
- take on roles from the text and be questioned about motives and intentions;
- use space and objects (including costume) in a variety of realist and symbolist ways to represent meanings in the text; to physically represent the psychic or cultural distance between characters, for instance;
- create 'missing' scenes or moments that are suggested but not fleshed out in the original text;
- explore how to use gesture to convey 'sub-text'; how inner speech can be visibly played, for instance;
- script, or improvise, alternative scenes or endings;
- demonstrate to each other that there can be a variety of 'possibles' when it comes to the interpretation and representation of meanings (different groups will respond to the same task in different ways).

Drama provides students with an immediate and physical means of getting to grips with texts and textual representation. Most of what our students know of the world, they know through representations of it. Drama provides students with a way of reconstructing the experience that is represented. This process causes students to become more conscious of 'voice' – the ideological interests of the text's producer.

In the *Green Children* lessons in the Resources section, the students begin with a story from the *Chronicles* about the appearance of 'fairy children' in Suffolk. Through the drama work they discover that the Chronicler's real purpose is to persuade his readers of the virtue of conformity and submission to the law. In a very concrete and physical way students can, through their drama-making, ask questions:

- Who is telling the story? (voice: dominant/marginalised; gender; culture, etc.)
- For whom?
- What form does the story take?
- What is emphasised/made invisible?
- How else could the story be told? (from other perspectives)
- What is the *real* story being told? (What are we being persuaded to think/feel?)

Drama and writing

Just as working in drama can help students to turn abstract ideas and written language into concrete and living representations, so it can also help students to translate lived experience into a variety of written representations. There are pragmatic and pedagogical reasons for encouraging this process. Drama, in its live forms, is the most ephemeral of arts. It exists only in the moment of performance. Written outcomes provide a permanent and visible record of a student's progress and learning in drama. Writing may also help students to reflect and deepen their response to drama they have made or watched. The drama itself may provide a logic and purpose for writing in genres that students might otherwise find tedious – reports, arguments, letters. In this table I have drawn on KS3 students' own reflections about how drama helps them with writing. The students were grouped in three ability bands based on an assessment of writing samples. While the charts focus on writing they also serve as a good general summary of how drama can help students in English.

Those students who are most challenged by writing responded particularly well to:

the non-threatening, 'can do', climate of the drama	Drama is a spoken art. Young people are at home with using interpersonal language in social situations – it is their most familiar experience of language. The student's exchange of meanings in drama is not as exposed to failures of technical accuracy as it is in reading and writing activities
collaborating on ideas and acting out in groups	Drama is a social art form. It is realised through collaboration. Young people support the development of each other's skills by pooling their resources and ideas in the drama – individuals have this social resource to draw on for their own written response
being able to use objects and furniture to represent places and ideas before describing them in writing	Selecting and using visual and concrete symbols is easier than using the abstract systems of symbolic language. Choosing the right piece of furniture for a character, deciding on a photograph that might symbolise an event or a memory gives young writers material to translate into writing
the story form of drama which held their interest	Narratives are a very familiar and accessible means of ordering and presenting experience. In drama the story is physically acted out and the tensions and emotions of the story are emphasised. The story of the drama together with its appeal can be used to provide a context for a specific piece of writing, e.g. trial notes, coroner's report, economic prediction
the chance to 'hot-seat' characters, i.e. to interview someone in role	Finding out about a character by asking questions and listening to and watching the responses the character makes helps students to differentiate and complicate their character descriptions. Seeing a character will flesh out, literally, the students own ideas

In the middle of the range students responded particularly well to:

the social realism of the theme and the form of the drama	Drama allows students to explore personal and social issues which are meaningful for them in the context of relationships – bullying, family politics, racism, personal identity. Students enjoy the realism of drama but also enjoy the tensions and heightened emotions. In drama, students explore the role of feelings in our thinking and doing

becoming emotionally engaged with the theme through the drama	Drama personalises abstract themes and concepts. A drama about racism will involve students in acting out or responding to the lives of those who are affected by it – they will feel for the characters in the drama as a means of coming to think more about the theme of the drama. Even if students go on to write an impersonal piece of writing – a school anti-racist policy for example – they will be charged with the emotions of the drama
discovering more about a character or situation through taking part in improvisations	Drama is always dialogic – made from many voices. Each role will see events differently and will respond differently. This helps students to see an event from a range of different points of view. Students discover more about their character from the way other role players respond to them. This experience helps students who are looking to include a wider range of perspectives and more fully rounded characters in their writing
negotiating first drafts for writing based on the experience of the drama	Drama represents social experiences, structures and processes. Students become involved in human situations which offer a wide variety of writing opportunities. A drama situation may produce letters, journals, legal documents, scripts, narrative. Students can negotiate their own writing from a wide range of alternatives and compare their chosen genre and register with peers who may have chosen a different form of writing based on the same drama situation
personal response/journal writing which allows for subjective responses to the drama work	Students enjoyed the social and collaborative nature of meaning-making in drama but also needed to interpret the drama for themselves, in their own individual voice. Personal response writing allows students to reflect on their feelings about the drama and to build personal interpretations of what might happen next
At the top end of the ability range students responded particularly well to:	
looking for sub-text in the gestures and action of improvisation	Students enjoyed building ironies and contradictions into their role play by using the non-verbal signs of gesture and space to counterpoint the language or to give it nuance. This helped students to think about referencing non-verbal signs in their writing – to describe the discomfort an apparently confident character is experiencing, for instance

recognising and introducing symbols and metaphors into the drama; being aware of the drama as an artistic text open to crafting and interpretation	Although drama is realised through interpersonal speech and life-like actions it is a textual form. Students enjoyed elaborating the drama as a text with layers of meaning, motifs, key symbols and themes. For these students involvement in the drama was very close to 'reading' and 'writing' in the literary sense. This experience helped students to think of structure and metaphor in their own writing
finding and using appropriate registers for writing based on the teacher's model of language used in the improvisation	Students enjoyed the challenge of writing in unfamiliar registers and genres of writing when these registers and genres were suggested by the logic of the drama and used by the teacher in role, e.g. writing in the voice of a boss, legal dispositions needed for a courtroom scene, imitating historical language and documents
being interviewed by others in role as a way of stretching their own understanding of the character they were playing	Articulate students enjoyed the challenge of being 'hot-seated' in role and needing to keep in role whatever they might be asked by the others. Having to respond to questioning intuitively and credibly helped to confirm the students' sense of a character and gave them material for character development in their writing
scripting scenes to be used in the drama, or having their writing used to further develop the drama	Writing produced in response to the drama can be reintroduced into the drama as a means of moving the action on. A letter written by a student might be read in role by one of the characters. A diary entry might be read out as a starting point for the next improvisation. Any form of document or written text can be used as part of the story of the drama

The living experience of drama

So far we have concentrated on the subject of drama: on the codes of production and reception, the histories and skills of drama, which exist independently of learners and which need to be acquired. The drama curriculum needs to be explicit in terms of what aspects of the subject will be taught, but it also needs to be explicit about the role that drama will play in the lives of students. The students are the subjects of drama in schools. Through making, performing and responding to drama, students are given the chance to discover more about themselves, other people and the world that they share. There is, then, the lived experience of the drama curriculum, which will be different for different students. Through their physical participation in drama activities and through their physical experience of drama events in the school students learn not just what drama is, but also what it does; the role that drama serves in our cultures.

In this sense, drama in schools is like the drama of traditional societies; it both reflects and makes community. In the past and in the present, communities have seen drama as performing important cultural and civic ends. Drama has been, and can still be, an important means of making the hidden influences of a community's culture visible, discussible and changeable. Drama represents how we live, how we have come to live this way, and how we might live differently. It both uses and comments on the webs of rules, conventions, status, traditions, collective identities, taboos and other shared meanings that constitute a community's culture. Making drama involves students in discussing and commenting on these cultural concepts. It allows them to 'play' with images of who they are and who they are becoming; to invent alternatives and to physically experience the difference of being 'someone else'. The production and performance of drama is also a form of community making. It requires a community (which might be a class or a school play production group) to work together towards a shared experience in which the communal goal is placed before individual interests.

The influence that drama might have on the culture of a school and its students is difficult to express in terms of concrete aims and objectives, but for many schools it is the most important contribution that drama makes. It is similar, in this respect, to sports. Both are social and physical activities. Both are valued for the contribution that they make to the students' physical, personal and social development rather than for vocational or academic reasons. Both involve the community and project the school's image through plays and matches. In many schools it is the *doing* of sports and the arts and the personal benefits that come from being involved that are valued above their importance as formal subjects.

As we noted earlier, a school's drama curriculum can and should combine local and national priorities. The common core of aims and objectives was a synthesis of guidance offered at a national level, but the lived curriculum needs to be locally defined and experienced. In general terms, however, there are three broad areas of cultural learning that students might experience in drama, or that teachers might aim to provide through their delivery of the drama curriculum. These three areas are: boundaries, public and private lives, and citizenship.

Boundaries

Whatever form drama takes it challenges us to explore, recognise and extend our physical, emotional and cognitive boundaries. The boundaries between what is me and what is not; what I feel confident to do and not confident to do; what I know about myself and others and what I don't.

The first boundary that students encounter is between watching and doing. Many students may come to drama with a strong sense of boundary between these two activities. To get up and physically participate in drama in front of one's peers is an important social boundary to cross. Students may also need to explore and recognise their own physical boundaries – what they are prepared to do and not do. Some students may be comfortable with realistic role-play but feel exposed, inhibited and vulnerable in dance or more abstract acting styles. Practical work in drama challenges the students to extend their physicality into more expressive and public behaviour.

Drama provides the space for students to explore their own identities – the boundary between what is me, what is other – through working on the problems of creating and representing roles and characters. Creating a character is a process of creating a fictional identity which is both different from and the same as oneself. When an actor plays Ophelia the character that we see physically on stage is not the actor herself, but it is also not-not the actor herself. We enter into role, we project an external image of another person but in doing so we bring something of ourselves to the character; this is why different actors can play the same character in different ways. In making and taking roles students discover that they will sometimes identify closely with the role they are creating and at other times they will strongly disassociate themselves from the role's attitudes and behaviours. These are concrete **acts of identity**. In drama, students have the chance to explore their emergent identities through reflecting on the acts of identification and non-identification that they make during the drama.

Feeling comfortable with experiencing and expressing emotions in public is also an important boundary to cross for many students. Schools are not generally conducive to such behaviour. Students themselves may be fearful of public expressions of feeling lest they should appear weak and vulnerable to their peers. The curriculum tends not to prioritise the engagement and expression of feelings in the classroom. The ability to feel, and to express feelings to others, is an important social and aesthetic quality.

Private and public lives

We all live in two worlds: the public and the private. The public refers to our social lives and public behaviour and the private to the intimacies of our family lives and our own solitude and inner speech. This distinction is of great importance in drama for two reasons.

In different ways, drama has shown us how people behave in response to the circumstances they find themselves in. This helps us to understand the extent to which our social lives are culturally constructed. In most public situations we have a set of cultural agreements about how we should behave and treat others. These agreements provide a framework of rules that are impersonal, i.e. expected of everyone. The language and behaviour of the courtroom is different from that of the dance floor. The more that students understand that so much of their adult lives will be spent in situations that require appropriate language and actions, the more prepared they will be to adopt (or challenge) the roles and responsibilities of public life. Drama can also provide students with an alternative experience of situations. If they take on the role of someone who is different from themselves in terms of status, gender, age or culture, they will also experience and use different language and behaviour.

Secondly, drama does not just represent the relationship between behaviour and social circumstances, it also comments on and interprets this relationship. The focus might be on revealing the oppressive circumstances that cause a young woman to accept an arranged marriage even though, privately, she doesn't want to. The focus might be on a specific aspect of situational behaviour such as status, environment, cultural difference. In order to explore the relationship between social behaviour and circumstances, drama often concentrates on the troubled margins between the public and the private, the difficulties caused by the interpenetration of the two worlds. One only has to think of the conflicts between private desires and public duties experienced by Macbeth, Hamlet and Lear. The most interesting place for students to explore the private and the public is where they collide. There have been frequent occasions when my life as a teacher has collided with my private life, and each occasion has generated enough material for several dramas.

Students are intensely aware of the distinction between the private and the public in their lives. Schools are public places which students need to negotiate. They understand the dangers of disclosing the private to the public scrutiny of their peers and their teachers. Sometimes these dangers seem so great to students that they will avoid any public behaviour in case it is read as a sign of the private, or leads to discussion of the private – the fear of answering questions or volunteering to help, lest you are accused of being a 'nerd' or 'teacher's pet'. In the classroom, teachers can contract and police a public world that protects the students' privacy while providing the rules, codes, manners to facilitate the involvement of students without threat. Elsewhere in the school, students may feel more vulnerable and less protected by formal agreements about behaviour. Drama can draw students' attention to the need to establish, among themselves, a set of rules for public behaviour in school that respects the privacy and rights of others; a highway code that allows all students to safely negotiate the playground.

Citizenship

There is an important relationship between the active participation in the public forum of drama and the active involvement of citizens in maintaining and extending democracy. Like participatory drama, democracies require the active involvement of citizens who are willing to put the common good before their own interests and to take whatever actions are needed to ensure the protection of the democratic virtues of equality, justice and freedom. Like drama, democracy is practised socially and in *public* – in debates, meetings, demonstrations, committees.

The roles that students take in drama at KS3 are often citizen roles. They are faced with problems, dilemmas or conflicts of interest in the drama that require them to act collectively rather than in their own private interest. The difference between what is best for me and what is best for the community is a dilemma commonly explored in drama. A drama may also challenge students to face the problems of difference. How do we decide what's best when we have so many different ideas and different people to consider? How would I feel about what is happening in the drama if I was of a different gender, age, ability, culture?

In some cases drama will directly serve democratic processes in the school. Drama might be used, for instance, as part of an anti-bullying strategy to provide a public forum for students to represent, debate and try out strategies for ridding the school of anti-democratic behaviours. The sacrifices of time and the personal responsibility to the collective that students take in order to be involved in a school play are also like the sacrifices that individuals must make in order to serve as citizens.

The roles, skills and knowledge of the drama teacher

In this section I am going to look at the roles, skills and knowledge of a drama teacher. My interest is in identifying what a potential drama specialist might need in addition to the skills and knowledge required of any competent and qualified teacher. All teachers, for instance, must have knowledge of the subject they are going to teach and know how to apply this knowledge in the classroom. They must be experienced in basic classroom management and planning schemes of work that are relevant and appropriate to the students they teach. They must know how to assess, report and record the achievements of their students.

This section assumes, then, that the potential drama specialist is starting from a base of good practice. The additional roles, skills and knowledge that a drama teacher must develop are not necessarily unique to drama. Teachers in other Arts subjects will also be developing similar competencies as will sports teachers who share a similar dual role as classroom teacher and extra-curricular tutor.

Roles

Manager

The drama teacher needs to be able to manage time, space and bodies and to do so in both the social dimension of the classroom and in the aesthetic dimension of the art-form. We have already noted that time, space and presence are the key elements of drama and that the study and experience of drama is tied to understanding, controlling and using these elements, in all their variety, to create drama.

But the elements of drama are also the problematic elements of the social encounter with students in drama lessons. In most other subjects, students enter into classrooms where space is controlled by the layout of desks and other furniture. Their movement around the classroom is restricted by the simple instruction to remain seated. Their behaviour can also be controlled by the use of text books and individual, silent study. 'Sit down, no talking, open your books at page 33 and complete the exercises. There is no need for anyone to get up, you're working on your own so I don't want to hear any talking'. The usual control mechanisms of the classroom allow teachers to work with individuals, to control groups and to quickly establish their authority. It is also the case that in most subjects even the most reluctant students can be pressured into completing work – either in class, at home or in some form of detention.

In contrast, the drama teacher usually works in large open spaces with large numbers of students in short periods of time. The space, the students and the teacher are the material for the lesson – it is rare to find drama being taught from textbooks in the conventional manner – it is a practical subject. Nor can students be forced to do drama – take roles and make enactments – against their consent. These characteristics of the drama lesson make additional demands on a teacher's existing classroom management skills. The mode of management that will be used is the **contract** and we will return to the skills of contracting later.

There are certain management principles that can assist teachers in making effective use of the time and space and physical behaviours of students in drama lessons.

Element	Principles
space	Make sure that the space for drama is clean, well prepared and cleared of everything but the essential furniture or equipment required for the lesson. Students will pick up on the signs the space gives them. If it is messy, dirty and neglected students will respond accordingly!
	Anticipate the problems the space might create. Begin lessons with a formal use of the space; have the students enter and sit in a formal circle of chairs (or on the floor) or have groups of chairs prearranged if the lesson begins with group work.
	Establish clear boundaries for student work; place groups yourself so that they are not too crowded or too distant; make corners, levels and dangerous space off-limits; insist on students working within the space that has been allocated so that they don't interfere with other groups.
time/tasks	Give groups clear objectives and an expectation of the outcome of group work. Set and keep to time limits for each group task.
	Anticipate potential problems of noise, aggressive behaviour and uncontrolled use of space and furniture by including constraints in the briefing for group work. I want you to ... I don't want you to ... This isn't an opportunity to have a fight and roll all over the floor ... I don't want to see anyone crossing over into another group's space ...

Consider carefully how a scheme of work will be broken up into lesson-units. Where do the natural breaks occur? How can the endings, beginnings and homework be used to strengthen links between lessons which may be a week apart? Begin lessons by having students recap from last lesson, end by anticipating how the work will develop in the next lesson. Give students questions to consider or homework related to the drama (e.g. writing in role, making a map or mask) between lessons.

Vary the experience of time so that there is an enjoyable and satisfying balance between the quiet, reflective and slow analysis of the relationship between time, space and presence and busy, energetic episodes when the drama may move forward more rapidly.

behaviour   Carefully consider the size and composition of groups in terms of gender, ability, friendship groups, power dynamics.

Develop an explicit contract that is a negotiated and agreed set of rules or 'manners' to control, protect and respect the students.

Use a variety of groupings within the lesson; whole class, small elective groups, small selected groups, pairs.

Make sure that you know everyone's name! It is difficult to control individual behaviour without being able to name the individual. Identify leaders or key players in the group and work with them to gain respect and interest.

Isolate disruptive or negative students either by careful consideration of groupings – dispersed or contained in one group. Don't allow one or two students to prevent the rest from working. Avoid confrontation in front of the whole class by organising group work while you deal with disruptive students privately; keep them out of the group work until they have accepted your terms.

Don't try to force students to do drama. In group work allow students the possibility of contributing to the making without having to perform themselves. Students are more likely to perform if they don't have to!

Animateur

In many schools drama is at best an optional activity that has a fairly marginal status within the curriculum. The role of the drama teacher will include being an animateur who seeks to develop drama in ways that begin to move drama from the margins to the core of the life of the school.

The drama teacher needs to be able to clearly advocate the unique contribution that drama makes to the curriculum. This will involve an assessment of the school's local priorities and how drama can make a direct contribution to them. We have already seen in the first chapter that schools place different values on drama – as a form of PSE or as an integral part of

English, for instance. The drama teacher is likely to have to enter into long and difficult negotiations to gain extra curriculum time, or manageable time-periods and appropriate spaces. These priorities are unlikely to be in place unless a drama teacher has worked to establish them! Negotiating a place and time for drama is made easier by forming partnerships with other 'sympathetic' subject areas; English, Art and Music, for instance.

The drama teacher is also responsible for animating opportunities for extra-curricular drama activities through the creation of lunch-time or after-school clubs. These are entirely voluntary and enjoyable opportunities for students to pursue their vocational interest in doing drama. Setting up, running and maintaining extra-curricular drama makes considerable demands on a drama teacher's time and energy, but there are clear rewards also. A different kind of relationship and loyalty is established in extra-curricular work which will transfer back into curriculum drama – you will have 'friends' in the classroom. Extra-curricular work also gives drama a very visible and public face in the school – drama is seen to be doing a good job and the students' commitment and sacrifices will be noticed. You are reclaiming the traditional role of drama as a living community practice that both reflects and makes community.

The community dimension of drama in schools and, therefore, of the drama teacher's role will extend into work that is done with, and for, other groups in the community that the school serves. Productions are a popular way of bringing parents and families into the life of drama. School productions have an irreducible community element. They are local productions made by students who are also known to the audience as sons, daughters, neighbours, sisters. The response to school productions is often celebratory and filled with positive community pride rather than objectively critical. Students are given the opportunity to project a positive image of themselves, the school and the community they belong to. The best production work also draws on the hidden talents and strengths of other teachers who are not associated with drama but who have skills in design, lighting, costume or stage management. Production work may also be targeted at specific groups within the local community – the local primary and special schools, pensioners' clubs and cultural centres such as museums or galleries.

The drama teacher is also responsible for providing students with living examples of drama through organising visits to the theatre and for bringing touring theatre and performance work into the school. Carefully chosen theatre visits provide the means of bringing all students into the culture of theatre-going. The theatre can only be accessible to all if all are given access to it through education in its conventions and practice in theatre-going. Theatre work that is bought in, or visited, should reflect the cultural diversity of aesthetic traditions in this country. Students should experience African and Asian performance in addition to the mainstream and avant-garde Euro-American tradition of theatre.

Facilitator

According to the Oxford Dictionary to facilitate is 'to make easy or less difficult or more easily achieved'. All teachers play the facilitator role: wanting to make it easier or less difficult for students to achieve their potential in a positive climate. Because drama is a social art that requires the physical involvement of its producers and because a class is already a social group that the students are physically involved in, the drama teacher needs to be able to facilitate the working dynamics of both kinds of group – the group that comes through the door and the group working together on the production of drama. There has to be a recognition and facilitation of the central paradox of drama teaching. The first condition of theatre is that it is *by choice*. In schools, particularly at KS3, students are often required to do drama. They have no choice.

There are three aspects to the facilitation of this paradox:

1. a clear and visible priority is given to the students' lived experience of the drama curriculum and there is a willingness to diverge from or modify the planned curriculum as a result of this experience;
2. the creation and maintenance of a regulated 'public world' in the drama classroom;
3. a high degree of tolerance and skill in managing and allowing student choices about the form and content of the work.

A practical drama lesson has to be planned in a way that allows students to become comfortably and confidently involved as the lesson progresses. The sequencing and staging of the learning process of the lesson – the realising of the objectives – has to be mediated through the imperative of making the students' lived experience of drama comfortable enough for them to want to join in. Whatever the planned objectives might be, students' inhibitions, physical embarrassment, fear of censure, transient moods and relationships to others in the group need to be taken into account.

The drama teacher needs to be able to make an accurate reading of the class as a social group, the individuals in the group and their relationships to the group as a whole. This is not a psychological reading, a guess at what is going on inside each student. It is an assessment of a group's culture and the social roles that students play within this culture. The drama teacher's concern is with the relationship *between* students; their public and social interpersonal behaviours. In their experience of the public world of school, individual students express their personal needs through the roles they choose, or are given, within the culture of the groups they belong to.

These individual needs might include the need:

- to belong
- to contribute
- for recognition
- for anonymity
- for status
- for power
- for dependency
- for freedom
- for recognition of particular problems.

The expression of these needs through 'role-behaviour' (behaviour that is specific to the group and to the classroom situation) may have both positive and negative manifestations. In the table that follows I have tried to categorise the social roles that students might adopt and to describe the positive and negative behaviours associated with the roles taken.

Positive behaviours	Social roles	Negative behaviours
Respond well to the responsibility of managing group work and getting the job done. Have the respect of others in the group. Once 'on-side' with ideas and objectives others will follow	**leaders**	Use their status within the group to challenge the teacher's authority. Others in the group are forced to choose between following peer-leader or following teacher. Gate-keepers who will prevent others joining in. Physically and vocally dominate discussion and practical work.
Willing to adapt to and compromise with others. Do not pursue their own need for power. Will accept direction from others and are satisfied with helping to realise another student's ideas	**followers**	Rarely initiate ideas or contribute to discussion and planning. Wait for others to get involved and take risks. Become 'stooges' for negative leaders. Develop a habit of non-participation. Fail to 'taste' leadership

Debunk pretentiousness; bring a raw, earthy and healthy disrespect to the work. Introduce ironies and parodic behaviour to lighten and relieve emotional pressure. Make the social experience of drama more enjoyable for all	**jokers**	Prevent or subvert serious, honest responses. Hide behind their humour. Ignore the sensitivities of other students. Distract groups from task. Distract the teacher with facile or petty physical and vocal responses
Can be trusted and relied on to fetch, carry, report, stay late to help out, send messages. The 'stage managers' of the group	**helpers**	Would rather help than do! Find other jobs to do while groups work on production of drama – cleaning out cupboards, stacking books. Seen as 'creeps'; compromise their own status within group
Get groups 'doing'. Help to move students out of their chairs into physical action. Keep the pace and rhythm of the class brisk and busy. Enjoy taking part and getting on with it	**doers**	Want to short circuit necessary discussion and planning. Commit too quickly to first idea offered. Impatient to show work before it is ready. Reluctant to watch and evaluate other groups' work
Have no positive role to play!	**negative spectators**	Remain on the outside of the work. Do not make any positive or active con-tribution but through body-language and insidious comments and asides seek to subvert the work of the teacher and the other students. Energy is expended on trying to make sure that nothing happens. May tease or threaten other students out of class for their willingness to be involved in drama
Sensitive and protective of the needs of individual group members. Monitor for signs of emotional distress or conflicts between the drama and other students' personal agendas. Sense and stand up for what is fair and just	**'sisters' and 'brothers'**	Over-protective and over-sensitive to the needs of others. May gossip or exaggerate personal problems. Raise personal or pastoral problems at inappropriate moments. Attribute personal motives for other students' choices of role and role behaviour in the drama

Make the teacher more conscious of group dynamics, individual needs. Resist cosy consensus and insist on individual difference and perspective	**loners**	Fear the social demands of drama. Suffer anxiety and fear exposure. Become more inhibited and more fearful of the public world because of their private experiences in drama class

Different teachers will have different ways of categorising and recognising the diversity of social roles in the class. And students don't come ready packaged into these roles!

There will also be local cultural and gender differences in the way that roles are played. But some awareness of the different functions that individuals play in the creation and maintenance of a group culture helps a teacher to

- manage the social dynamics
- allocate responsibilities
- support and challenge appropriately and
- facilitate the social production of drama.

Drama both reflects and *makes* community. In its social production of drama the group will reflect its actual strengths and weaknesses, its patterns of power and domination, its habitual responses, its social health. But the way in which the teacher facilitates the social production of drama will make a difference to the class as a social group; there will be positive effects which are transferable to other social situations faced by the group.

In trying to accentuate the positive and eliminate the negative in social role behaviours the teacher may use a wide range of facilitator functions. The practical nature of most KS3 drama work means that some of these functions are related to ensuring the production of high quality work during the lesson. The social nature of production in drama means that some functions are related to maintaining the social health and working effectiveness of the group. Below I have summarised what some of these task and maintenance functions might be.

Facilitator functions	
Task-related	
initiating	proposing tasks or goals or actions, defining group problems, suggesting procedures
informing	supplying relevant facts and instructions, giving expression to feelings or opinions
seeking	asking for information, opinions, feelings, ideas from others to help group discussion and practice

clarifying	interpreting ideas or suggestions, defining terms and tasks, checking out group or individual issues
summarising	putting together related ideas, restating suggestions, offering a decision or conclusion for group to consider
testing for reality	asking the group to test what it is doing or saying by referring to known facts or source text in order to see if the group is behaving realistically/authentically
expediting	prodding the group to action or decision, encouraging groups to strive for quality in their work
Maintenance-related	
harmonising	attempting to reconcile disagreements, reducing tension, getting students to explore and respect differences
gate-keeping	helping to keep communication channels open, facilitating participation, suggesting procedures that permit open sharing of agendas
consensus testing	testing a group's willingness to agree and the basis of such agreement – is it owned by the group or dominant individuals?
encouraging	being firm but friendly, warm and responsive to positive behaviour, indicating by facial expression or remark the acceptance of students' positive contributions
compromising	offering a compromise when own idea or status is in conflict with group's, modifying planned lesson in the interests of group cohesion or growth
process observing	watching how groups operate and sharing these perceptions with the groups
standard setting	expressing standard for the group to work by, testing behaviour against such standards
trust builder	accepting and supporting openness in group members, recognising and reinforcing risk-taking
interpersonal problem solver	promoting open discussion of conflicts between group members in order to resolve conflicts and increase group cohesiveness, involving group in maintenance and enforcement of contract

Actor/dramaturge

Making and performing drama is at the heart of the drama curriculum. In some cases the drama will be based on the realisation of an existing playtext (script/dramatic literature), in others the drama will be devised from the exploratory work of students and may be based on a non-dramatic source such as a story, poem, image or abstract theme. In both forms of drama there are two kinds of text in play: the **source text** and the **performance text**.

The performance text – what is actually said and done in performance – only exists in the time of performance whereas the source text remains. In our everyday experience of theatre we are conscious of the autonomy of the performance text every time we go to see a different production of a familiar work of dramatic literature. Our interest is in what a particular director and group of actors will *do* with a familiar text that might be different or that might offer a fresh interpretation.

In the modern Western theatre tradition two tendencies have developed in the making of performance texts. In the first, the producers (directors, actors, designers, etc.) are concerned to offer an authentic interpretation of the playwright's intentions – the performance text is a direct representation of the playwright's instructions to the producers (script, stage notes and directions contained in the original written score). In this literary form of theatre the audience judges the extent to which the performance text is 'faithful' to the original written score.

In the second tendency of performance text-making, the source text is only important in so far as it provokes or begins the devising of a performance which is as much a representation of the producers' own ideas and agendas as it is of ideas and agendas suggested by the author of the source text. The source text (where it exists) may be adapted, abridged, even subverted. The performance text may be built out of fragments of text from a variety of sources. If the literary tendency highlights the playwright as 'author', then this alternative tendency highlights the producers as 'auteurs'.

The term **dramaturgy** is used to describe the weaving together of stage actions into a unified performance text: its roots are in the Greek *drama-ergon* – the 'work of the actions'. A performance is made out of 'actions'; not only what is said and done but also the sounds, lights, and changes in space. Even objects become actions in performance in the sense that they change the space they are placed in. But of course the 'actions' are not all simultaneously present – they are temporally and spatially sequenced to make a performance that unfolds in time. Dramaturgy, therefore, refers to the sequencing of actions both at particular moments in the performance and in the larger scale relationship between moments which 'taken together' comprise the whole experience of a complete performance; we experience each passing moment of a performance but we also experience the developing structure as it gathers towards a sense of a 'finished' performance (which is the total and progressive effect of all the actions that together constitute a dramatic statement or experience).

This is the art of drama as a genre of performance rather than as a branch of literature – the intentional weaving together of stage actions in order to make a living and lived *experience* for an audience. At KS3 the drama teacher, as dramaturge, has two responsibilities: to initiate and develop the 'weave' of the drama, and to draw students' attention to that 'weaving' so that they begin to share in the teacher's knowledge and to make their own decisions about the 'weave'.

The weave that the drama teacher makes with students is dependent on **knowledge** of a wide variety of dramaturgical devices or conventions drawn from both theatre traditions and also from film and TV conventions. It is also dependent on the skills of **structuring**, which refers to the ways in which the various conventions may be assembled and juxtaposed in order to create an aesthetic and educational experience for students. The role of the drama teacher as dramaturge is to use knowledge and the skills of structuring *responsibly*.

The teacher is responsible for:

Developing and enhancing the artistic potential of students' ideas and responses

While discussion, negotiation, planning and researching are all important activities that go on in drama as they do in other subjects, the teacher's prime responsibility is to facilitate the move into using the codes of theatre production as the main activity in drama. This means being able to translate the students' intentions and suggestions, or the subject objectives for the lesson, into dramatic ideas and processes. To see, for instance, how discussion about human experiences can become a dramatic realisation of imagined experience – roles, situations, gestures, symbols, contrasts – or to choose dramatic literature that is appropriate to the needs and interests of the students.

In mainstream theatre the actor is the prime signifier. Whatever else is used in terms of props, costume, lighting and spatial design it is principally the actor who draws our attention and who generates and communicates dramatic intentions and possibilities. Students at KS3 are unlikely to have the trained body of an actor or to be able to match the expressive powers of an actor. The teacher needs to make greater use of props, lighting, sound and other non-physical properties to reinforce and support students as actors. The teacher may also use her own skills of acting as a model of status and register:

- to demonstrate a character's response to the given circumstances of the dramatic context;
- to initiate role responses, or to offer cues for other actors to follow;

- to transform (through her own physical and psychic transformation into character) the actual world of the classroom into a fictional world or context.

The uses of 'teacher-in-role', as a dramaturgical device, is one of the most important contributions that drama education has made to the world of theatre.

Managing the constraints of time, space and numbers

As well as aspiring to art-making the drama must also take account of the logistics of the lesson – the time available, the limitations of the space provided and the need to actively include as many students as possible in the drama.

This consideration, in part, accounts for the difference between dramaturgy in the classroom and in other genres of theatre. The relatively short duration of a drama class has meant that drama teachers have developed particular conventions that can be quickly produced without the need for lengthy preparations or rehearsal tableau, improvisation, hot-seating, etc. Using these conventions a teacher can provide students with a variety of different activities in the space of a single lesson.

Space is one of the elements of drama but many lessons have to be taught in classrooms or small spaces which don't permit movement or a creative use of space. In these circumstances the dramaturgy has to focus on time and role and an imagined, or mentally constructed, 'picture' of space to make drama.

Few mainstream plays make use of thirty or more actors working as an ensemble! The drama teacher has to structure in a way that allows for every student to be involved. This may involve varying the size of groups, rotating or doubling-up key roles or organising group work so that different aspects or episodes of the narrative are worked on simultaneously. The advantage of having six or seven small groups is that they will produce a range of different responses to the drama – *different* tableaux, roles, situations, etc. This range of difference is a positive aspect in the dramaturgy.

Balancing the planned curriculum against the local needs and lived experience of students

Working with students in the classroom is very different from working with actors who are either professionally or vocationally motivated. A director can expect professional actors to deal with their emotional responses to the material that is being dramatised. S/he can also expect actors to attempt what is required and to accept critical feedback during rehearsal and performance and to maintain professional working relations with other actors. The same cannot be expected of students.

In drama education the students often need to be lured or persuaded to take part and the teacher needs to carefully consider the level of personal challenge that the work presents. The students' actual emotional responses to the material that is being dramatised often becomes the focus of the work. The subjective feelings that students experience become the basis for their emotional understanding of the material and the human experience it suggests. It is this subjective understanding, which in other styles of acting leads to an objective characterisation, that is of interest to the teacher.

Drama is a powerful medium for exploring and representing human experiences. The teacher needs to use it responsibly so that students feel stretched but not threatened by the emotional intensity of the work. The teacher needs to respect students' vulnerabilities and insecurities about using their bodies expressively in front of their peers and to understand that problematic relationships in the class are unlikely to be put on hold for drama.

Skills

Questioning

Drama is a questioning medium. It seeks to disturb, extend or change our understanding of who we are and who we are becoming. Drama tends to focus on those moments of experience which forcefully reveal the paradoxes and ambiguities of human actions and reactions; those moments which provoke us to ask questions about ourselves and the worlds in which we live.

In order to respond to these questions, students use a logic based on their prior cultural and narrative experiences. In other words, students' responses to the questions raised by a drama may draw on their knowledge of similar narratives and how they can be expected to turn out and they may also draw on their existing cultural understanding of how people are likely to act and react in the given circumstances of the drama. It is the teacher's responsibility to help students to operate these logical systems and to apply them to the drama as it unfolds. Through questioning the teacher helps students to make sense and make connections. The teacher's questions also reveal differences and ambiguities in the student's responses. In the social art of drama, meanings are not privately held or formed, they are established collectively through debate and through the dialogue that is established by the teacher's questioning of the sense-making that the group does.

The questioning of the human condition that underpins drama flows through the modes of making, performing and responding.

In *making* drama, students work at discovering and exploring both the means and the meanings that will form the dramatic representation of a particular experience. The relationships between character, context and action, and dramatic conventions are forged through detailed research that corresponds to the rehearsal process in mainstream theatre. Theatre work which is based on extensive exploratory rehearsal is sometimes referred to as **laboratory theatre**. A theatre in which dramatic means are used to research, test and develop our understandings of human nature and culture. To create a character, the young actor must ask questions about what will make the character recognisably different from the actor's own character. How do I communicate this 'otherness'? How will this 'other' person respond in ways which are psychologically, culturally and historically true to the given circumstances of the drama? This making of character will also raise questions for the young actor about the parameters of their own identity – how would I respond in the same circumstances?

In *performing* drama, students seek to convey their understandings and findings through characterisation and actions which are selected as being concrete examples of their ideas about the experience that is being represented. These examples of character and behaviour provoke the 'W' questions (see below) that an audience seeks answers to as the drama unfolds. In the modern Western theatre tradition, we deduce the inner lives of characters from the external gestures and visible responses that the actor selects as being 'significant' of character. The patterns of gesture and response that the actor creates are often inconsistent or paradoxical or surprising so that the audience is left with complex questions about why people behave as they do and how they are shaped by cultural circumstances. Actors may behave 'as if' they were someone else in another time and place, but only so as to raise for the audience the open-ended question – what if ...?

In *responding* to drama, students need to ask the questions that will help them to unravel the human puzzle that is presented on stage. When we see a play performed for us, we make sense of the drama that is being presented through piecing together the clues and cues that answer our questions:

questions

What is happening?
Who is involved?
Where and When is it happening?
What has happened to create this moment?
What will happen next?

The drama teacher works alongside the students, using questions to discover the sense they are making of the dramatic experience. Without asking the drama teacher cannot know what individuals think, how they respond, what connections they are making with their own experience or what ideas they might want to try out. There must be a genuine attempt by the teacher to see the dramatic experience from the students' perspective – to understand and work within their view of the world. This projection is not unlike the projection that producers must make in order to ensure that the meanings of the drama are communicated effectively to an audience.

The questions that are selected might fulfil a variety of functions in the drama lesson:

Clarifying: checking students' responses; confirming where students are with the drama; checking that instructions have been understood

Inferring: asking how the gestures and actions the students are using are tied to the 'meanings' which they want to communicate; checking out the teacher's perceptions of the work with the students

Probing: drawing students' attention to the consequences or implications of their actions/ideas; testing commitment or understanding; pushing students to deeper levels of engagement

Challenging: checking prejudicial or culturally specific attitudes or ideas; questioning the social dynamics of the group; encouraging the group to go beyond the surface of experience

Reality-checking: asking the group to test their ideas or work against their own sense of reality and logic.

Different questions elicit different responses from students. There are obvious distinctions to be made between open questions which do not predetermine a response and closed questions which contain assumptions about the response expected. The root word of a question will also determine the response that is made. Below I have categorised different root words in questions and the responses they are likely to get:

What ...?	*asks students to itemise or list –* what do you need? What is X scared of? What will his daughter say when she finds out?
When/where/which?	*asks students for specific information –* When is this happening? Where would she sit? Which of these two chairs would make the best throne?
How ...?	*asks students to reveal processes and feelings –* how are agreements made in this family? How would she feel about what he is doing? How can we represent that idea?
Could/would ...?	*tests potential –* Would she still come back after all she has heard? Would you behave in the same way yourself? Could you imagine that it might be different?
Should ...?	*asks for moral judgement –* Should he have spoken to his mother in that way? Should anyone make that demand on another? Should we try and listen to each other?!
Why ...?	*asks for explanations –* Why doesn't she answer the question? Why is the king so angry with his daughters? Why are you finding it so difficult to play the character?

Contracting

We have already noted that students can't be made to do drama in the same way that they can be made to write or to complete textbook exercises. There has to be an agreement to do drama. This agreement is easier to make if there is a visible and negotiable framework of ground rules, codes of conduct and behavioural objectives. The framework serves the same purpose as the rules of a game. The 'players' know that the rules of the 'game' provide a safe and fair means of becoming involved. Knowing what to expect from others and what is expected of you gives confidence, security and protection. Knowing what the rules are and what happens if you, or others, 'cheat' removes the fear of getting it wrong. In every classroom teachers will use an agreed sanctions system to protect the climate for learning. The contract in drama may include the sanctions system but it is more than that – it represents an ongoing dialogue about how to maintain the quality of learning and interpersonal relationships in drama.

'Dialogue' implies that students are also contributing to the contract. They have the opportunity to protect themselves and to establish a culture for the drama class that will make it safer for them to engage with the drama-making.

The concerns that students might have will include what will happen if:

- people laugh at me?
- no one wants to work with me?
- I reveal something that might be used against me?
- no one listens to my ideas?
- I feel uncomfortable about my body?
- I just don't feel like it today?
- people in the group ignore me, or disrupt my work?
- the drama touches a raw nerve?
- the drama disturbs my cultural beliefs?
- I don't agree with what we're doing?

These are all possibilities which the drama teacher needs to be aware of and to discuss with the group. This discussion might lead to decisions and social agreements about what will happen if any of these concerns emerge. The nature of the concerns that students might have results from the particular characteristics of making, performing and responding in drama.

Drama requires trust, trust involves taking risks

Contracting recognises the risks involved for both teacher and student and seeks to limit the risk by defining and proscribing behaviour which will break teacher–student and student–student trust.

Drama requires the public presentation of private states of being or feeling

Actors need to express a wide range of emotions, but the peer and institutional culture of schools seeks to suppress or censure expressions of strong emotions. Contracting legitimises and protects the expression of feelings and recognises that the emotions that students express as characters are not to be read as signs of the actor's own character! If the actor is required to cry it doesn't make the actor a 'cry-baby'!

Drama draws attention to the actor's use of body to physicalise meanings and therefore attention is drawn to the actor's body

The actor's fictive use of the body is the central signifier in drama. Contracting rejects the idea that you must look like, be the same age/culture/gender as, the character you will physicalise – anyone can take any part. Contracting also disallows comments about other students' bodies and allows students to discuss their own tolerance levels in physically demanding work.

Drama is socially produced; individuals are asked to put the common 'good' or goals before their own private interests

Drama belongs to the public sphere of our lives. Just as in other public, or civic, practices we are asked to observe certain conventions and to put the communal needs and goals before our own private interests. Contracting stresses the need for us to work for the good of us all rather than to pursue personal agendas and priorities.

The drama seeks to make connections with the public self and the private me of the actor and the audience

We see ourselves in the drama; its representations may seem to touch on our most private and intimate lives or comment on the presentation of self as bully or victim or cheat. Contracting ensures that all activity in drama is masked – there is no need to declare or probe into the private world of the student.

The teacher's contracting in drama may serve different pedagogic purposes:

Framing	*Setting the parameters of student/teacher behaviours* – use of space, noise levels, productivity levels, clarifying objectives, courtesies, and sanctions system
Anticipating	*Pre-empting likely problems* – talking about specific control/space/personal and interpersonal problems likely to be encountered in the work
Trouble-shooting	*Applying the contract* – defusing and managing breaches of contract by referring back to the agreements that have been made and asking for them to be complied with (the contract becomes an impersonal regulator)
Taking collective responsibility	*Sharing the maintenance of the contract* – open discussion of problems and breaches of contract with expectation that class, as well as teacher, are responsible for settling difficulties.

There are two important considerations for any teacher who wishes to establish contracting as a means of classroom management:

1. *Start as you mean to go on!* It's important to establish contracting with students as soon as they enter the new school at KS3. The behavioural problems of 11-year-olds may not seem as difficult to manage as those of 14–15-year-olds. Firmly establishing a contract at the outset will prevent problems emerging later in the student's career.

2. *Never give up!* It takes time to create a learning community in which individuals regulate their own behaviour and negotiate the climate for learning.
   Pulling a group into shape can be a long and difficult process – but you
   have to hold on to the vision that contracting offers! Why else be a teacher!

Structuring

Some of the work that a drama teacher does will be in the form of lessons that
are planned in ways which would be familiar to teachers of other subjects –
lessons on aspects of theatre history, stage craft or technology for instance. But,
as we noted in the discussion of the teacher's role as dramaturge, there is an
expectation that making and experiencing drama is at the heart of the drama
curriculum.

The quality of the making and experiencing is, at first, dependent on the
teacher's skills of structuring. During KS3, the teacher's modelling of structure
and the choices that are available in structuring a dramatic experience will
merge into the expectation that the students will become increasingly
confident, knowledgeable and responsible for their own structuring.

In a conventional lesson plan, activities are organised so that students can
understand, internalise and apply the particular skill, concept or knowledge
that is contained in the lesson's objectives. On the surface, a planned drama
experience may look like a conventional plan. The teacher will have aims and
objectives for the session and will also have a list, or sequence, of activities for
the students to engage with. But, in addition to satisfying the curriculum
objectives for the lesson, the sequence must also provide students with a living
experience of drama – an analogous experience to being in or at a play or
watching an episode of drama in some other form. The sequencing of the
lesson needs to be as subtle and as crafted as any other dramatic sequence that
is planned to unfold its meanings, or theme, in time and space and which
moves the audience, progressively, towards a new-felt understanding of the
human issues and themes that are being dramatised.

In this sense the structure of the classroom drama is in the form of a
montage: a construction of meanings which is a specific result of the assembly
of form and content during a drama. The montage, or the juxtaposing of the
'pieces' used in the drama, also guides students through the dramatic event or
experience. The montage is more than the linear sequence of events in the
narrative. In theatre, the events of the story are only one dimension of the
presentation. Theatre is a spatial as well as a temporal art. What happens in
the theatre space, in terms of objects, design, lighting, sound and the physical

arrangement and gestures of the players also contributes to our under-standing of what is happening. The montage that comprises the practical component of a drama lesson, then, refers to the totality of all the actions in the lesson and it is assembled, as in any dramatic event, to produce specific effects.

In some lessons (particularly in early KS3) the students may be aware of following a story where the sequence of the lesson is tied to the stages of the story – beginning, middle and end – and which focuses on causal relationships between people, contexts and events in the story. In other lessons, the story may already be known or the source material for the lesson may not be in the form of a narrative. In such cases the structure of the dramatic montage is more visible. The various activities and tasks are assembled in such a way that students' attention is drawn to themes or ideas which develop and deepen as the work progresses but without being driven by a narrative logic. A tableau representing a particular moment in the story might be followed by students giving 'thoughts' to the characters in the tableau, or rearranging the figures in another group's tableau to demonstrate an alternative perspective – this sequence is designed to develop understanding of the human themes and issues without moving the narrative forward. The actions extend out from a moment suggested in the narrative, the lesson progresses in time, but the dramatic exploration is held to this moment in the narrative.

In most forms of drama the montage is notated, or recorded, as a sequence of **scenic units.** These units may correspond to the playwright's own division of the play into scenes. They may also correspond to the director's, or actors', division of the play into units which correspond to the development in the actors' performance or the emotional rhythms of the play. The study of the different ways in which theatre practitioners have and do construct montage and the relationships between different genres of theatre (comedy, tragedy) and different approaches to montage will be the focus in drama for students in KS4 and beyond.

However the montage is made, the scenic units must have meaning in themselves and also contribute to the complex meaning of the play as a whole. In other words, each unit must have its own logic for performers and audience, but also contribute to the logic of the whole performance. The concept of 'episode' is a useful construct for students to understand. They will know, from their experience of TV drama, that an episode of a TV series should make sense in itself but they also know that their understanding of characters and the 'meanings' the producers want to communicate accumulate over a number of episodes. So there is the sense of the episode both having its own shape and logic but also contributing to a developing understanding which will only be complete when all the episodes have been watched.

Each scenic unit or episode of the montage provides a 3 – dimensional experience for actors and audiences – it is not made of a single action such as a change in space or a line spoken, it is a complex of simultaneous actions that together offer meaning.

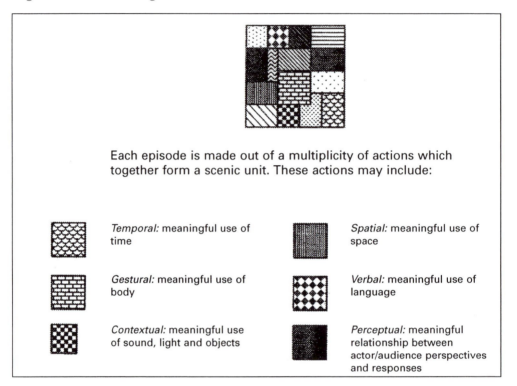

Each episode is made out of a multiplicity of actions which together form a scenic unit. These actions may include:

Temporal: meaningful use of time

Spatial: meaningful use of space

Gestural: meaningful use of body

Verbal: meaningful use of language

Contextual: meaningful use of sound, light and objects

Perceptual: meaningful relationship between actor/audience perspectives and responses

In drama education the division into scenic units may correspond to the exercises, tasks or improvisations that together constitute the lesson. The lesson plans in the next section of this book have been organised in such a way – the complete lesson plan represents the instructions for the montage as a whole but it is subdivided into units which, in my mind at least, make sense in themselves while also contributing to the students' progressive understanding of the themes and ideas in the drama as it unfolds and moves from one unit to the next.

In most forms of drama there is a specific requirement that each scenic unit will be played in the dramatic present. The dramatic present refers to the particular quality of time in drama. We appear to be producing, or witnessing, a 'here-and-now' representation in which events unfold as we see them – they are not reported past events as they are in story. But in effect the 'here-and-now' of drama must be linked to what has already happened or what we already know prior to this moment in the performance. The 'here-and-now' of drama must also imply a future or cause an audience to question how the events we are witnessing now will create future events. It is this sense of an implied future (or destiny), which is connected to past events through what is revealed in the events that are happening now on stage, that differentiates the dramatic present from the 'here-and-now' of everyday life. The present in drama is always in the margins between a tangible past and future.

The linking between the past and an implied future in each passing moment of the drama causes the audience to extend and deepen their understanding of the play's theme. Each passing moment should build on and clarify what has happened and clarify, through implication, our expectations of what will happen next.

In the diagram below, the boxes represent the episodes, scenic units or other divisions in the drama. The boxes are linked by the narrative, or thematic, thread that guides us through the drama. The arrows indicate the way in which the audience's understanding of the play's themes extends and expands as the drama progresses. Each scene implies the future while extending, confirming or confounding what has previously been revealed or implied.

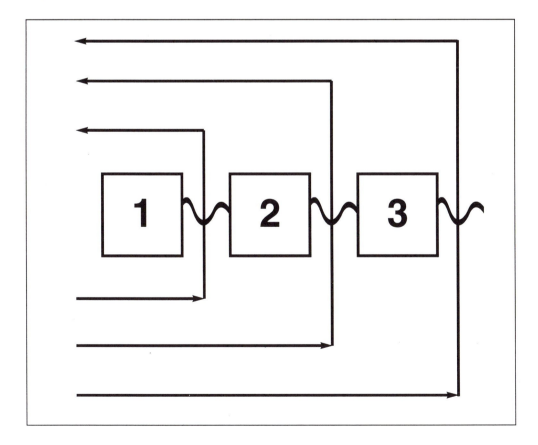

There may be further aesthetic considerations in making the montage. The relationship between scenic units may be used to create different kinds of rhythm. The **rhythm** of a drama may be tied to an emotional score – a balance of 'highs and lows' – or to the tensions in the relationships and events that are being represented. The rhythm in school drama, as in some forms of theatre, may create a balance between **efficacy** (where the purpose of the drama is to bring about some kind of change in understanding and attitude or to create lasting results for the participants) and **entertainment** (where pleasure and fun are given precedence).

The use of the elements of drama (time, space, people, objects, sound and light), the structuring concepts of 'montage' and scenic 'units', and the principles of playing a 'dramatic present' are common to both conventional theatre presentation and to curriculum drama at KS3. However, the drama teacher has additional concerns that guide the structuring of curriculum drama and which, inevitably, make such drama appear 'different' from some other forms of non-school theatre. These considerations include:

Working positively with the constraints of time, space and numbers

Drama is a very flexible art form but even so, drama teachers often work with constraints that are quite unique to the school situation. The time allowed may vary from regular weekly slots between 45 minutes and an hour or more in length to shorter and/or less frequent periods. It is difficult in such circumstances to maintain the progressive experience of a montage. The time constraints may mean that students are forced to engage and work with drama more quickly and sketchily than in other forms of non-school drama. The spaces that are used for drama may vary from custom-built studios to corridors! The drama teacher is also working with a large number of actors who can't be expected to be mere extras to the work of star individuals – they must all be offered a meaningful and varied experience of producing drama.

Managing the planned with the lived

We have noted that curriculum drama differs from other forms of drama in the sense that it is not 'by choice'. Engagement has to be negotiated. Structuring in curriculum drama must take the lived experience of students into account in terms of their inhibitions, differing abilities, peer-group dynamics. The need to deliver a planned curriculum in drama that is related to the school curriculum and ethos as a whole is also a constraint on structuring. The teacher does not have a free rein. She is responsible for ensuring that lessons are productive, well ordered and supportive of the school's ethos. There is often a greater emphasis on the efficacious uses of drama (to produce specific results) than on providing entertainment (as important as the experience of pure pleasure in the theatre is).

Working with two aesthetic traditions

The principles and concepts of structuring that we have discussed are derived from the restricted art of literary theatre. They describe the way in which practitioners in conventional, 'serious', theatre approach their work. But, as we have noted, most students' aesthetic experience and knowledge is derived from the oral and communal aesthetic of film, TV and other forms of popular entertainment. Structuring in drama should not alienate students from their own cultural knowledge and practice – it should seek to build bridges between aesthetic traditions.

The principles that follow may help you to positively address these considerations – which are particular to the local context of making, performing and responding to drama within the curriculum.

Teach structuring through the experience of structure

Make the montage – the assembly of form and content – visible to students; discuss the choices that are being made; encourage students to use, and reflect on the use of, the full range of drama elements so that their own group work is three-dimensional.

Co-author to create co-ownership

Encourage suggestions about how to develop both the plot and the montage of the drama; work with and from the students' questions about the themes and ideas that are being dramatised. Use (and therefore pass on) your own skills and knowledge to enhance students' work – sound, lights, choreography and direction where appropriate.

Introduce and use a diversity of conventions and traditions

Introduce and blend together conventions from other cultures and from film/TV. Avoid suggesting that there is a hierarchy of conventions in which the conventions of Western theatre have a 'natural' superiority over other traditions.

Prohibit unacceptable images

Art in school is restricted to representations and messages which are acceptable to the whole school community – student-artists are not free from censorship. Have no concerns about either banning, or confounding, prejudicial images and characterisations.

Use an episodic structure

This needs to be open-ended like the episodes of a TV series; each episode speaks for itself. Don't be tied to having to finish the story or to complete all the stages of a planned sequence. An episodic structure gives greater flexibility – you can extend or shorten the sequence of episodes according to the needs and interest of the group. Episodic structures are a familiar means of bridging the time gap between one episode and the next, cf TV series, soaps, etc.

Use group work to cover more ground

Whenever possible give groups *different* tasks or scenes to do in order to cover more ground; stress difference; make watching more interesting. Encourage groups towards diversity of meaning rather than conformity. In terms of the response to group work, encourage students to extend their sense of 'possible meanings' rather than to reproduce the same ideas.

Stress the communal rather than the individual, and structure accordingly

Draw attention to the means and meanings used in group work rather than to comments about individual contributions and skill levels. Structure for ensemble work rather than principal characters – think of groups of characters rather than individuals. Run group presentations as a single performance sequence so that reflection is on the *whole* experience created by the group as a whole.

Practical drama work in schools often takes on a conventional structural shape **(genre)**. For instance, when I was trained to teach drama the genre we were given followed a conventional pattern of games/ice-breakers, short improvisations or scenes, followed by de-briefing and relaxation exercises. Whatever the content or objective for the lesson we would try and fit what we were doing into this pattern. Nowadays there is a greater variety of genres of practical drama to be found – greater variety means greater choice for teachers and students. In the table that follows I have tried to identify some common genres of drama work and to offer some advice on structuring within each genre. I have tried to avoid creating a hierarchy of genres by giving greater value to some rather than others. It is my belief that all of these genres are needed in order to effectively deliver the practical component of the KS3 drama curriculum. I have, however, given extra consideration to the

conventions approach because it is the genre that works best for me and I believe it to be particularly appropriate to KS3.

small group play making	*Students prepare their own scenes based on a title or theme. The work is performed to the other groups.* • Break the production process of the scene into stages (beginning, middle and end, for instance) and give instruction and feedback at each stage • Give opportunities for reworking scenes after feedback • Focus on helping groups to clarify *what* is being communicated and *how* it might be communicated more effectively • Encourage students to explore non-naturalistic conventions in their work, e.g. dance, masks, narration
rehearsal	*Students work on extracts or whole plays and are given responsibility for a full realisation, or performance, of the playwright's work. Through a process of rehearsal students are expected to explore the meanings communicated by the playwright and how to codify those ideas in theatre form.* • Encourage creative approaches to rehearsal by using other drama conventions such as improvisation, sculpting, 'tableau' or 'hot-seating' to research character, setting and language • Don't leave it to the students – they need direction and knowledge from you! The students rely on you to make sure the finished work will not embarrass them! • Be flexible with casting, use multiple characters or double-up or have different actors for different scenes • Encourage students to use the full range of the elements of drama – light, space. objects – to comment on, or reinforce, the verbal playing of the text
skills development	*A particular skill, such as movement, voice, dance, mask-work or improvisation, is isolated and taught to students who then practise in order to improve their expertise. Practising may involve following the teacher/trainer, private or group practice and applying the skill in a short game or exercise.*

- Establish the relevance of the skill to the drama work; how students will use it, how the training will help them to do better drama
- To feel comfortable in a skills-based exercise (such as learning to move in a mask so that the mask is always facing the audience), students may still need some sense of context and content. Drama is a concrete art in which players need a sense of real-life motive and purpose
- Use the students' strengths, focus on skills of agility, speed, dexterity and imaginative response – but avoid the fear of physical embarrassment!
- Use popular cultural forms as vehicles for skills development: rap, juggling, acrobatics, dance, ball games

living through	*Students, working with the teacher-in-role (a player in the drama), place themselves in an imagined situation and then, through making and taking characters, they behave as if they are living through the imagined experience as it unfolds. How they act and react is determined both by the 'culture', or given circumstances, of the situation and also by agreed narrative characteristics such as elements of fantasy or an intensifying of the potential 'drama' of the situation.*

This is a very action orientated genre. Quite literally, nothing will happen unless the participants take action themselves. In this way students are very conscious of forging their own histories through their actions, just as Shakespeare's characters were.

The development of this genre of theatre experience is closely associated with the work of Dorothy Heathcote and Gavin Bolton, but 'teacher-in-role' is also linked to the 'joker' in Augusto Boal's 'forum theatre' and to the old tradition of adults joining in and enhancing children's fantasy play. This genre is often used as a model for drama in KS1/2.

- Spend time constructing the context of the imagined situation – the 'W' questions
- Use teacher-in-role to initiate, model, guide and control the students' behaviour; weave together the students' responses; build atmosphere; work as a storyteller within the story

- Encourage students to create and try roles and role responses that are different from their own daily roles and behaviours
- Break the work up and include reflection, exercises and other conventions in the montage so that both the theatre and the analysis of behaviour offered by the imagined experience is not forgotten

conventions approach	*A 'laboratory theatre' approach in which some aspect of human behaviour or experience is isolated and selected for close exploration. The aspect may be contained in a playscript, a literary source or any text that comments on human nature/culture. The montage is made of episodes in which students use a variety of techniques or conventions to illuminate the content. An initial tableau of events may be followed by hot-seating characters or providing inner monologues for the initial tableau. The techniques used are derived from conventions which are local to curriculum drama – teacher-in-role – as well as from post-naturalist theatres – alter-egos, Brechtian devices, forum theatre.*

- There must be an aesthetic logic to the montage: it's not enough to simply use a bag of different techniques – taken together the various exercises and techniques used must develop into a complete and satisfying dramatic experience
- Look for opportunities to layer the work by combining conventions or reusing earlier work. We might provide the soundtrack of memories for a poignant moment that is caught in tableau, or repeat lines spoken earlier as we watch characters react to hearing them again
- Don't move too rapidly from the use of one convention to another. Look for opportunities to use new conventions to further develop or investigate the students' work; rearrange the spatial relationships in a tableau, for instance, to see how the meaning changes, or, focus on a particular action or gesture and isolate it for discussion or as the basis for further creative extension

Knowledge

This will be the shortest of the sections, even though it ought to be the longest! It isn't possible to 'give' the knowledge that a drama teacher needs in these few pages. I am restricting myself to describing the different categories of knowledge and giving some sense of what might be included in each. (I have included only knowledge that is specific to drama teaching – not the basic body of pedagogic knowledge that all teachers need to acquire). Part of my own pleasure in teaching drama is knowing that I will never know enough – I need to constantly seek new knowledge that will enhance my practice. The breadth of knowledge that I describe here will take experience and time to gain. The knowledge is to be found through reading the books suggested in the annotated bibliography and beyond. It is to be found through going to the theatre and cinema as often as possible and through going to workshops. It is also to be found through experience, both of teaching drama and of being attentive to the world around us.

In order to be an effective subject specialist in drama at KS3, a teacher needs to acquire knowledge in these five categories: *practical, theoretical, technical, historical, cultural*. There will of course be overlap between these categories – masks are placed in practical knowledge because there are traditions and particular uses of masks that teachers should know about, but technical knowledge is needed in order to teach mask-making.

At first glance the knowledge that is described may seem to go far beyond the requirements of the KS3 curriculum. Certainly, you don't need everything that is here to be a drama teacher at KS3. But the more knowledge you have of drama yourself the more you have to draw on and inform your teaching at any key stage. In the English educational system, a drama specialist is required to have knowledge equivalent at least to A-level.

Practical knowledge

- dramaturgy; the use of the elements of drama to communicate meanings
- acting styles, dance, masks and other relevant aspects of stage craft
- management of personal and interpersonal behaviour
- project management (production).

Theoretical knowledge

- specific to teaching drama in schools (books like this one, for instance)
- dramatic theory (which might range from the works of Aristotle to Raymond Williams and the theoretical writings of Brecht, Stanislavski and others)
- semiotics of drama (how meanings in theatre are constructed, communicated and reconstructed by audiences)
- theatre anthropology (the different cultural uses and manifestations of performances in other times and places as well as our own)
- the theoretical writing of key twentieth century theatre and school drama practitioners (which might include Slade, Way, Heathcote and Bolton but also Stanislavski, Meyerhold, Brecht and Boal)
- awareness of relevant critical theory – feminist, post-colonialist, performance, literary.

Technical knowledge

- sound and light technology
- use of IT as control system for above and for use as part of drama (using the World Wide Web for research, for instance)
- scenic design and construction (including costumes and properties).

Historical knowledge

- major periods and styles of Western theatre – Greek, Elizabethan/ Jacobean, Realism/Naturalism, Symbolism and Expressionism
- twentieth century and pre-twentieth century playwrights, e.g. Shakespeare, Jonson, Brecht, Miller
- genres of tragedy and comedy
- key periods of social history – e.g. Athenian and Elizabethan societies, Industrial Revolution, 1930s and 1960s
- popular theatres and entertainment, e.g. mysteries, commedia, melodrama, vaudeville, federal theatre project, musicals.

Cultural knowledge

- major non-European performance traditions, e.g. Kathakali, Noh and Kabuki, Carnival, shadow puppets
- contemporary trends in writing and performance styles
- media and representation
- major cultural movements such as modernism and postmodernism
- the oral and communal aesthetic tradition.

Resources

Year 7 – Green Children – the real story

Context

This structure is designed as a bridge between forms of drama making that may be familiar to students in KS2 and the new challenges of drama as a separate subject at KS3. The drama is built around an enigmatic account of the discovery of fairy children in the twelfth century. The structure begins with a sequence of 'story games' which could be applied to any narrative. These games are intended to give the students clear objectives and an 'easy-to-follow' framework for groups to follow. The advantage of story games such as these is that they allow students to move around inside the story and to begin to discover its themes and ambiguities for themselves. The students then move into a sequence of work that moves from participation based on rules and game objectives to participation based on frame – the given circumstances of the story.

The structure is intended to teach students about:

- the differences between game and frame
- characterisation
- the use of basic conventions such as tableau, teacher-in-role, and soundtracking.

The structure also introduces students to familiar dramatic themes:

- issues of cultural identity – culture vs Nature
- voice (whose voice do we hear?)
- gender difference and expectations.

The full structure requires *three hours* of drama.

MYSTERY OF 24 GREEN BABIES BORN IN US!

Two dozen green babies have been born in Massachusetts and Rhode Island over the past year, all to mothers who are vegetarians.

Secret reports by health authorities reveal the first green baby, a 7 pound, 2 ounce baby boy was born on August 28, 1993 in Boston – and similar looking infants have been born throughout the area over the past year.

All of the babies are reported to be in excellent condition, except for their green skin from head to toe.

Shocking

Until now, health officials have tried to keep the story hushed up for fear it would create panic among pregnant mothers and endanger the lives of their unborn children.

But bowing to relentless pressure from *Sun* investigative reporters, the shocking story of the green babies is being revealed here for the very first time.

Woodstock

When the first green baby was born, doctors were completely baffled by its skin – until they questioned the mother and learned she was a strict vegetarian.

The mother, identified as Sunrise Ankarra, 25, told doctors that she had been raised that way by her parents who were 1960s hippies.

'They were part of the Woodstock generation, and they lived in a commune until I was five years old,' says Sunrise.

'Everyone there was a vegetarian and I was taught that it was a sin to eat red meat. I never even ate a cheeseburger in all my life.

'But now I kind of wish I'd grown up eating meat like everyone else – because I never dreamed my baby would be born all green.'

Doctors say Sunrise's husband Jeremy, 27, is also a vegetarian, and has not eaten meat since 1991. But it was mainly due to his wife's vegetable-enhanced chromosomes that they produced a green baby.

Broccoli

Medical researchers say all 24 green babies shared one thing in common – they were all born to vegetarian mothers who consumed extraordinarily high green leafy vegetables during their pregnancies.

'It's extremely important what the mother eats during pregnancy because that's what the baby is using as the building blocks for its body,' says Dr Steven Baumgartner. 'In all these cases, the mothers had far too many green vegetables, especially broccoli, in their systems – and that's the main reason why their sons and daughters are green.

'The mothers could also have drunk water with a high copper content during their pregnancies and it's a scientific fact that copper turns green when oxidised. Most likely the high copper content came from the rusty pipes in the old homes where they live.

All healthy

'But there's no doubt that babies like this are exceedingly rare. Over the years we've had many babies born with bluish and yellowish skin and of course we knew how to proceed with their medical treatment. But this rash of green babies was something far out of the ordinary. Fortunately all the infants are 100 per cent healthy, although they will most likely have green skin for their entire lives.

'But their vital organs are in fine working order and that is the most important thing, As they grow up, all the green babies will have to be shielded from the sun because they don't have enough melanin in their skin to withstand long exposure to sunlight.

'They'll never be able to go sunbathing at the beach like other people, but otherwise I foresee no problems.

'One thing is certain. They won't have to get made up for St Patrick's Day, and that's a big holiday here in Boston.'

(Boston *Sun* – 13 September 1994)

1. Work in groups on the newspaper story about mysterious green children. Read the story carefully and then discuss whether the story is true or not. You could make two lists – one which has reasons why the story might be true; the names of the parents, for instance. The other list will include reasons for thinking the story might be false; it's in the *Sun* newspaper, it sounds like the plot for an episode of *The X-Files*, for instance. Discuss your findings with other groups. **20 mins**

2. Look carefully at the language of the newspaper story. How is the story made to sound 'scientific'? How are vegetarians described? What does the story consider to be 'normal' and what does it suggest is 'abnormal'? Discuss what you think the real story might be – is it a practical joke, or an attack on vegetarians, or a scare story? **10 mins**

This is an optional sequence that might be done as part of an English or Media lesson. It is an interesting exercise in itself that introduces students to the ideas of voice, bias, probability, cultural prejudice. Crucially, it reminds students that stories have sub-texts – that the real story might not be the obvious one. It also sets things up nicely for what follows!

The second story was written in the thirteenth century as a 'chronicle' or record of history. A 'chronicle' was like a modern newspaper; it provided news and information for the people of the time.

Green Children

Two of the early chroniclers tell a strange story about some fairy children who were found near Wolfpit in Suffolk at the beginning of the twelfth century. They were a boy and a girl like ordinary people in size and shape except that they were light green all over. Some country people found them lying dazed and frightened at the mouth of a cave. They talked in a strange language and did not seem to understand anything that was said to them, so the people took them to a knight, Sir Richard de Calne, who had a castle at Wikes. They seemed very hungry, but they would not touch bread or meat, only cried bitterly. At last by chance some broad beans were brought into the house, and they seemed eager for those, and when people opened the pods and showed them the beans inside they ate them hungrily. The boy was sad and weak, and soon pined away, but the girl learned to eat human food and to speak the Anglo-Norman language, and in time she lost her green colour and looked like everyone else. She was christened, and when she grew old enough she was married and settled down. People asked her how she had come there, and she told them something about her country.

*S*he said that the land they lived in was called St. Martin's Land, and the people there were Christians. There was no sun or moon but a kind of twilight like that before sunrise. All the country and the creatures in it were green, and the people were pale green too. One day they were watching their flocks when they came to the mouth of a cavern, and a sweet sound came out, the chiming of distant bells, which they had never heard before, and they followed it on and on till suddenly they turned a corner and came into the full light of the sun. The dazzling light and the rush of moving air dazed and stunned them and they fell on the ground. Then they heard loud voices and they tried to run away, but they could not see their way in the dazzling light, and they turned to and fro until the people caught them. At first they were very frightened, but the girl soon understood that they meant to be kind, and in the end she settled down into their strange ways.

3. Work on the story in a group. Make a list of the seven or eight key moments in the story – finding the children, taking them to the castle. Put your list into sequence – where does the story begin? When you have your list of events from the story, find a space and choose someone to be the 'storyteller'. The storyteller uses the list to retell the story – but the rest of the group have to act out the story as it is being told! The storyteller will need to include plenty of details and actions for the group to follow. Whatever is included in the story – sheep, knights, weddings – *must* be acted out! All the groups will work at the same time – it's a fun activity and you might not want to have an audience watching! **15–20 mins**

In order to work with the 'meanings' of the story the plot needs to be separated from the 'telling'. As soon as students begin this exercise they will discover that the story has two beginnings and that there are other paradoxes and contradictions within it. They must resolve these in order to move on. The exercise has helped them to see that everything is not quite right in this story. The acting out is fun but it also requires students to translate the story into a dramatic narrative, in other words into *actions*. If the storyteller doesn't use actions nothing will happen! The actors are encouraged to explore the basic conventions of physical theatre, i.e. everything that is physically present can and must be physically played!

4. Make groups of four and number each person *1–4*. When the teacher gives the signal to begin *1* starts to retell the story of the Green Children; after a few seconds the teacher shouts 'Change!' and *2* has to carry the story on without a break until the teacher shouts 'Change!' again and then *3* takes over. You then replay the game in the roles of characters from the story. Try telling the story as:

- the villager who first found the children, talking to other villagers
- the Green Girl, now a mother, telling her children the story of how she was found
- Sir Richard telling the King and his court what has happened in his village.

When you finish the game, discuss the following questions in small groups and then report back to the class:

- How has the story changed?
- What happens when it is told by different characters?
- What did you add, or leave out? **15 mins**

> The second exercise encourages the students to elaborate and change the details of the story in order to entertain those listening – a key storytelling skill! – it also begins to introduce frame by putting the listeners into role as well as the story-teller. The frames also suggest different registers of language according to the status and relationships involved. The use of different voices is a very clear way of demonstrating that every story has a voice and that the voice will tell the story in its own interest! Students will also discover the difference between first-hand accounts (the villager and the Green Girl) and second-hand reports (Sir Richard).

5. You have been asked to provide an illustration for the story. Which is the best moment to illustrate? In groups make a *tableau* to represent the illustration you think would be the most effective. Give your picture a caption from the story – 'She was married and settled down', for instance. Look at each other's pictures and try to guess the captions. What do the pictures tell us about the story? **15 mins**

6. What happened when the Green Children were first found? Who found them and what were they doing? In groups of eight, prepare a 30-second scene showing how the children were found and the villagers' first reactions. The scene should be mimed – no words! When the scenes are complete, pair the groups and as one group show their scene their partner group has to provide all of the sound effects to go with it – every sound (voices, animals) has to be reproduced. What were the different ways in which the villagers responded to the children – fear, anger, compassion, curiosity? **15 mins**

> The first exercise uses a basic convention to help students to isolate and select the dramatic material in the story: the first finding, the refusing of food, the death of the Boy, the dilemma of the Girl, the power of the lord, for instance. Tableau encourages the students to use the full range of drama elements – time, space, presence, objects, etc. – to communicate their understanding of the moment they select. Students should be encouraged to discuss the choices they have made in making their tableau and the choices made by the other groups.
>
> The second exercise changes the rhythm of the work. It asks the group to begin to think about characters and to begin to establish the *difference* between characters that will be needed for further dramatic exploration. The 30-second rule is unlikely to be observed by either the mime group or the group providing the soundtrack – you may well end up in a situation where both groups are improvising beyond the planned – always an interesting place to be!

7.   Divide into pairs and find a space to sit with your partner; decide who will be *A* and *B*. When the teacher gives the signal, *A* becomes the Green Girl who is telling her friend, *B*, about her first year in the village. The 'friend' helps by asking questions – How did she get used to the food? Does she miss her own land? Does she get on with the other villagers? After a while the leader will give the signal to change roles. *B* becomes the Green Boy and *A* becomes his friend – What has the year been like for him? Discuss the differences between the Boy and the Girl after a year. **10 mins**

> This exercise gives the students a 'private' space with their partner – some students will feel more comfortable in pairs work than in speaking out to the whole group. It invites the students to use their understanding of the story so far as a springboard to beginning to contribute their own imaginings to the story – it starts to become 'our' story. There is also an open invitation to express complex feelings and to project into the experience of the central characters. If it's appropriate you can 'spotlight' groups by moving around the pairs and asking each pair to share, briefly, some of their conversation as a performance for the others.

8.   Form a gossip circle. What are the rumours circulating about the Children? Each student invents, passes on or exaggerates what is being said among the villagers – are the Children angels or devils? Are they to blame for natural disasters, crops, sick animals, drought? What should be done with them? Discuss and use the results of the gossip to make the next scenes. **10 mins**

9.   Work in four groups:
      (a) the parents of the village
      (b) the carers: those who might have looked after the Children – doctor, priest, cook, teacher and friends
      (c) the children of the village (but not infants!)
      (d) the farmers and market traders; those whose livelihoods or work might have been affected.

What are the *different* ways in which your group might react to the Children. Among the parents, for instance, there may be some who are suspicious, caring, angry at the attention the Children receive, worried about their Children catching the Green Boy's 'disease'. Make a short scene that shows an incident involving your group and the Children – their first day at school, perhaps, or the day they were taken to the cattle market. After each scene the 'audience' can discuss the Children in their roles as parents, children and carers. **30 mins**

> The pairs work and the gossip circle will generate a bank of ideas and suggestions about the Green Children's lives in the village. The scenes require students to isolate and select an event that is representative of their view of the Children's lives. The stress on 'difference' helps students to create scenes in which characters will play out differences of opinion, conflicts of motive and intention. Students should be encouraged to think about and then play a particular objective in the scene; to blame/ protect the Children; to arouse suspicion; to show jealousy towards the Children.

A teacher-in-role alternative would be to work in four groups in which there are the two children and their carers or adopted parents in the village. Each group prepares a scene which is then played out with the teacher-in-role. The four scenes are:
- Parents call for doctor because Boy will not eat, teacher as doctor arrives and suggests forcing the Child to eat; how far will the family go?
- Parents call for priest because Girl wants to go to church and claims to be a 'Christian'. Teacher as priest shows more interest in Boy; does he recognise/respect the Cross? Is he the devil's work?
- Parents are preparing to take Children to the travelling fair which has come to the village; teacher as fairground owner arrives and tries to buy the Children from parents to exhibit at the fair – will they sell?
- Parents bring Children to the market so that they can choose food they like; teacher as angry parent confronts them because they have been playing with his children and his animals are now sick.

10. Sir Richard returns to the village at the end of the first year. He wants to know all about the Green Children and how they have got on in the village. What will the villagers say? Will they have different attitudes to the Children? Sir Richard calls all the villagers to his castle to discuss the Children's futures. Teacher takes the role of Sir Richard. Sir Richard leads the meeting of the villagers who must now decide what will happen to the Children.

- Can they stay? What if some villagers don't want them to?
- Will the Girl be allowed to marry when she is old enough?
- Is the Green Boy's 'illness' catching?
- What happens if more Green people come to find them? **15-20 mins**

This moves the structure into the 'living through' mode of drama. Everyone at the meeting behaves 'as if' they were living through the meeting as it occurs and unfolds. But the students have been well prepared in terms of contextual information, characters, events and differences of objectives. The teacher as Sir Richard has to manage the meeting – but he has the power of life and death over the villagers! He should probe and knit together the responses to confuse, confound and make more complex. He should either reinforce or go against the grain of the 'futures' implied in the previous scenes. He should also work to give the meeting a real sense of atmosphere and tension so that it is a powerfully felt experience for the students as actors.

11. Place two students as the Green Children at one end of the space – possibly in positions from earlier tableau work – ask the other students to think about their character's attitude to the Children. If they want to help and protect the Children they should stand close to them. If they care for the Children but are not prepared to look after them themselves they should stand further away. If they are suspicious of the Children, or don't really want them there, stand further away still. If they would be prepared to get rid of the Children because they bring evil, or ill fortune, they should stand as far away from the Children

as possible. Teacher asks a sample of students (as villagers) to declare why they have taken their position. Teacher asks those at either extreme 'How far would you be prepared to go to protect/destroy the Children?' Teacher pushes for a life or death commitment!

The scene is now formalised as a strategy game. Those who are prepared to destroy the Children themselves walk, very slowly, towards them. When they meet students in their path they stop. There are three courses of action; hold up a fist (fight), an open palm (talk) or stand aside. If open palm, students have brief chance to talk and then make decision again. If there are more fists than palms, the talkers must either stand aside or be prepared to die. If any student feels the urge to move at any time they must shout 'stop!' and explain before moving. The purpose of the exercise is to ritualise what would otherwise be a fight and to show that it is those who sit on the fence who must first face up to, or surrender to, the aggressors! **15-20 mins**

The students are using space to represent differences and conflicts among the villagers. The formal game structure provides a means of experiencing the drama and tension of the moment without it degrading into a brawl. The experience of realising that you would probably be one of those who stood aside and let the aggressors through is often a powerful moment of identification or non-identification for students.

---

12. There are many different versions of the Green Children. There is still a place called Woolpits in Suffolk.

- Why is it such a popular story?
- Do you think the story is true?
- If not, what is the real story that is being told?
- What are the reasons why the Boy dies and the Girl survives?
- What does the story say about what is expected of girls and who and what is 'natural' and 'normal'?

Discuss your ideas about the real story that is being told and share with the other groups.

Extensions

- Devise your own play of the story for a younger audience.
- Make a picture story book for younger readers.
- Rewrite the story from the point of view of the Boy or Girl; a villager.
- Rewrite the story as it might appear in today's *Sun*.
- Turn the story into an episode from *The X-Files*. How would Scully and Mulder deal with the case?

Learning outcomes – What have students learnt from the structure?	Subject objectives – Which objectives have been covered by the structure?
to consider and identify issues of voice, bias and cultural prejudice in a variety of genres of narrative	see appropriate objectives in the English curriculum
to play story games and to use the basic dramatic conventions of tableau, role play, small group play making, teacher-in-role	1.1 Learning about the creative and symbolic use of the elements of drama – time, space, presence, light, sound and objects – from their own experience of drama and from watching drama 1.3 Learning to recognise and name the conventions and techniques used in drama and something of their history, e.g. monologue, tableau, role-play.
to work in a variety of social groupings and to take some responsibility for aesthetic and task organisation	2.1 Learning to negotiate with others in a group and to adapt and accommodate to other people's ideas 2.2 Learning to work as part of an ensemble – acting and reacting to others
to take on and work in roles that are 'different' from their own; and note that effective drama depends on there being a 'difference' of perspectives	3.1 Learning and using a critical vocabulary for discussing drama, e.g. gesture, symbol, tension, rhythm and pace, contrast 3.4 Learning to distinguish and comment on the relationship between role codes and performer codes in drama

Year 8 – The Identification

Context

This structure is based on a well-known poem by Roger McGough. There is an interesting paradox between the awful tragedy of a boy's accidental death and his father's apparent lack of emotional response to the news. The setting of the poem in a mortuary appeals both to the ghoulish and to those who are familiar with the genre of hospital dramas on TV. The structure gives students greater responsibility for making (aesthetically crafting) their own contributions to the drama. The emphasis is now on students communicating their ideas to others rather than on the teacher creating a dramatic experience for them. The purpose of the group work is to encourage students to develop their own ideas about who 'Stephen' is. There is no suggestion that the group are working towards a single interpretation of the poem; rather they are being asked to use the poem as a springboard for exploring and representing ideas about socialisation, parental and peer relationships.

The structure is intended to teach students about:

- recognising and playing the text and sub-text of the poem
- transforming a source text (stimulus) into a performance text
- keeping options open in devising
- creating a fully realised dramatic sequence (making montage)
- matching form and content (means and meanings)
- working with text.

The students are working with these dramatic themes:

- conflicts between the private and the public
- father/son relationships
- characters who are shaped by cultural circumstances

The full structure requires 2.5 hours drama

The Identification by Roger McGough

So you think its Stephen?
Then I'd best make sure
Be on the safe side as it were.
Ah, there's been a mistake. The hair
you see, its black, now Stephens fair...
Whats that? The explosion?
Of course, burnt black. Silly of me.
I should have known. Then lets get on.

The face, is that a face I ask?
that mask of charred wood
blistered, scarred could
that have been a child's face?
The sweater, where intact, looks
in fact all too familiar.
But one must be sure.

The scoutbelt. Yes thats his.
I recognise the studs he hammered in
not a week ago. At the age
when boys get clothes-conscious
now you know. Its almost
certainly Stephen. But one must
be sure. Remove all trace of doubt.
Pull out every splinter of hope.

Pockets. Empty the pockets.
Handkerchief? Could be any schoolboy's.
Dirty enough. Cigarettes?
Oh this can't be Stephen.
I dont allow him to smoke you see.
He wouldn't disobey me. Not his father.
But thats his penknife. Thats his alright.
And thats his key on the keyring
Gran gave him just the other night.
Then this must be him.

I think I know what happened
 ... about the cigarettes
No doubt he was minding them
for one of the older boys.
Yes thats it.
Thats him.
Thats our Stephen.

1. Make groups of five to seven and elect a reader. Listen to the poem and share your ideas about what is happening in the poem. List your first responses to the poem under three headings:

   • *What do we know?* This column is for the facts. For instance, the boy is called Stephen. There has been an explosion.
   • *What do we guess has happened?* This column is for ideas that are suggested, or hinted at, in the poem. For instance, that Stephen's father doesn't seem to know what he was really like, or that Stephen may have had secrets that he kept from his father.
   • *What do we want to know?* Use this column to list any questions you might have about the poem. For instance, was Stephen responsible for the explosion? What kind of friends does he have? Where is his mother?

When you are ready compare your lists with other groups'. Are you all agreed on the facts? **20 mins**

The poem is the source text which the students will use to devise their own performance texts. In this first stage the students are given a way of deconstructing the poem so that it can then be reconstructed as a performance text which is both an interpretation and a commentary on the themes and ideas in the original poem. The headings are bound to lead to heated discussion about what is known and what is inferred. The only way of resolving different opinions is by close reference to the text itself. The questions heading creates an agenda for the work that is based on the students' own curiosities and wonderings. This is a reflective exercise which could also have used *iceberg* or *role on the wall* to the same effect.

2. Now that Stephen is dead, how will he be remembered? Will his friends remember him in a different way to his dad? Work in four groups, let each group take responsibility for making a different tableau/freeze-frame from this list:

    • Stephen as his father *would like* to remember him
    • Stephen as his friends *do* remember him – what did they used to do together?
    • Stephen as his Gran *would like* to remember him
    • Stephen as his teachers *do* remember him – perhaps he wasn't as obedient as his father thinks he was.

Look at each of the pictures and discuss the different ways in which people might have seen Stephen. Why didn't his father know more about him? Why is he so surprised to discover that Stephen may have been in trouble? **30–45 mins**

The purpose of this exercise is to highlight the sub-text of the poem – the difference between who Stephen is and who his father thinks he is. The performance of the images should follow the order given above so that *would like to* remember images are juxtaposed with *do* remember images. The exercise is deceptively simple. The students will be familiar enough with making tableaux, but now there should be an expectation that they will be more complex and selective in their composition. How succinctly can they capture all the nuances of the father/son relationship in a single image, for instance? Each of these images also touches on important areas of the students' own personal and social politics – of family, friends, parental expectations. Give plenty of time to the sharing of the tableaux and where possible work with them by using other conventions..
For instance, are there opportunities to:
• create the thoughts of the characters?
• rearrange the father's image so that it represents Stephen's real image of his family?
• arrange the characters in space so that we can see who is close/far apart and talk about what the distance is between characters?
• in the friends image consider how the peer-group dynamics change if we change our idea about which figure in the picture is supposed to be Stephen.
• look at the teacher's image and add to it Stephen in the classroom at age 7, 11, 14, 16 – how does he change over time? Put in images of teacher at these different ages – what does our work tell us about the process of education?

---

3. Divide into five groups and give each group a different verse of the poem to work with. Decide where Stephen's father is when he is speaking, who else might be there with him? How would the father speak the words – with anger? or sadness? or confusion? Would he speak softly? slowly? with long pauses? or perhaps quickly – rushing through his words? Let each group decide how best to play their verse. Allocate roles in the group and present the verse as a scene in which Stephen's dad is speaking and the other people who are there are listening and reacting to him as he speaks (you may choose to give some of the lines to other characters if you wish. You can only use the original words, you cannot add any new ones. You can repeat or abbreviate the text if appropriate). When the class is

ready you can organise the scenes so that they follow on from each other to make a performance of the whole poem. **30–45 mins**

Encourage students to think carefully about the match of 'means' and 'meanings'. Some groups may work in a hyper-realist style borrowed from programmes such as *ER* or *Casualty* in which they try to authentically reproduce the circumstances of a hospital mortuary. Others may work in a more expressive way – letting the body of Stephen speak, or using alter-egos, masks or sculptured figures, or using flashbacks from Stephen's life. The structure of the poem will give the performance its logic or through-line. The experience of the performance will be enhanced if there is a variety of different performance styles used by the groups. The verses should be properly rehearsed and have clear openings and endings.

4. How would the story of Stephen's tragic death be reported in the newspapers? Let the five 'fathers' from the previous exercise find a place to sit. The rest of the class are newspaper reporters sent to interview the father. What questions would they ask? How would they treat the father? What would be the best way of getting information from him. Go in groups to interview the 'fathers'. During the interview, you must try to get a photo for the front page – will the father let you take the photo? When you have finished the interview, get into groups and discuss what you have found out and how the newspaper should tell the story – is there an 'angle' you could develop? You might want to write the story, or mock up the front page for tomorrow's edition. The photos will need captions that will appeal to your readers.

Discuss with the 'fathers' how they felt about being interviewed and whether they think the press have been fair and supportive in their coverage of the story. **15 mins**

A definite change of rhythm is produced. The students move into 'living through'. The 'fathers' will experience actual disturbance when confronted by the press; their feelings will give insights into dramatic situations where private grief becomes public speculation. The reporters should be briefed/debriefed by the teacher in role as local editor.

5. How did the explosion happen? Go back into the four groups you used for the freeze-frame. Each group prepares a 30-second mime showing how the explosion might have happened. Watch these scenes. Each group is going to be given responsibility for providing a soundtrack for another group's scene. While we watch each group's mime again we hear the soundtrack provided by another group who are watching. The soundtrack is spoken in the words of the following:

    - the police officer's report on what the police think happened
    - the doctor's report describing the injuries and how they happened
    - the lie that Stephen told his father about where he was going
    - the story of what happened told by one of his friends who was there but who survived. **2 + 20 mins (+ homework)**

This is one for the students! They have worked carefully and in detail to create the performance of the poem, so this exercise gives them the chance to have some fun. Allowing comic elements, particularly playing with time by speeding up or slowing down action, should be encouraged. The soundtrack may need some research; watching and noting the language used in hospital and police TV drama for instance. The montage of mime and soundtrack uses the film convention of speech from one event (the coroner's inquest) played over action from another event (the circumstances of the explosion).

6. Imagine that Stephen's death is part of a new storyline in a soap opera. How would it be treated differently according to which soap it is? Think about, and/or act out, the different treatment it would get in:

  - *Byker Grove*
  - *Grange Hill*
  - *EastEnders*
  - *Brookside.* **1 hour**

This is an optional exercise that gets students thinking about the dramatic structure of popular soaps. They should work in 'loyalty' groups so that there is expert knowledge of the chosen soap. They will need to make explicit their understanding that soaps would give a different emotional weight and treatment to this kind of storyline. They should also plot out how the storyline would be seeded and developed to a conclusion over several episodes.

Learning outcomes – What have students learnt from the structure?	*Subject objectives –* Which objectives have been covered by the structure?
to distinguish between text and sub-text and how to play sub-text in a variety of ways	1.1 Learning about the creative and symbolic use of the elements of drama – time, space, presence, light, sound and objects – from their own experience of drama and from watching drama 3.2 Learning to identify and evaluate the different choices that can be made in drama that lead groups to make different interpretations/representations of the same material
to create a fully-realised dramatic presentation based on a source text	1.2 Learning how to use and control the elements of drama; particularly the body in space 2.4 Learning how to direct the work of writers, actors and designer into a coherent dramatic statement

how to use rehearsal techniques and dramatic conventions to explore and represent issues relating to personal and social identities (private and public)	1.3 Learning to recognise and name the conventions and techniques used in drama and something of their history, e.g. monologue, tableau, role-play 1.5 Learning to use a variety of processes to devise and perform drama, e.g. improvisation, workshops, rehearsal, scripting, storyboards, characterisation
to make connections between different genres of drama, including film and TV conventions	1.4 Learning to identify and distinguish historical and current genres of drama, e.g. tragedy, comedy, mime, mask, physical, soap opera 3.1 Learning and using a critical vocabulary for discussing drama, e.g. gesture, symbol, tension, rhythm and pace, contrast 3.2 Learning to identify and evaluate the different choices that can be made in drama that lead groups to make different interpretations/representations of the same material

Year 9 – Wedding?

Context

Devising a dramatic statement or sequence based on a stimulus is a common form of assessment task for students taking GCSE drama. The stimulus used here is a small ad that was placed in my corner shop – a found text. A woman advertises her own wedding dress and rings. This particular event is used as the basis for a thematic exploration of our cultural expectations of love and marriage. By mixing small-group exercises with whole-group performance and interactions, the structure allows groups to devise their own coherent performance texts within a communal context.

This structure is intended to teach students about:

- dramatic structure and play-building
- the actor's use of sign and gesture in Naturalist and Expressionist theatre
- how to play a 'dramatic present' (referring to what has happened/will happen)
- alinear devising processes
- gestus and symbol.

The full structure requires three and a half hours of drama

1. Look at the examples of children's playground chants. Songs and rhymes like these are a part of everyone's childhood. They are sung for fun and to play hand-clapping, circle or skipping games to. Can you work out the rhythm of each of these songs? Can you imagine what game might be played with each

one? These songs all refer to love and marriage – but what do they teach young children to expect from love and marriage and what images of the roles of men and women in love and marriage do they project?

Can you remember any playground chants or games from your own childhood?

Can you remember any that referred to love, marriage; what boys are/do; what girls are/do; sex?

Work in groups to recreate a chant and game either from the examples given or from your own memories of childhood. **20 mins**

Stands a lady on the mountain,
Who she is I do not know.
All she wants is gold and silver,
All she wants is a nice young man.
Madam will you walk,
Madam will you talk,
Madam will you marry me?

No!

Not if I buy you a nice armchair
To sit in the garden when you take the air?

No!

Not if I buy you a nice silver spoon
To feed your baby in the afternoon?

No!

Isabella, Isabella, Isabella, farewell,
Last night when we parted,
I left her broken-hearted,
And on the green mountain
There stands a young man.
Choose your lover, choose your lover,
Choose your lover, farewell.

Open the gates, love, open the gates, love,
Open the gates, love, farewell.

Go to church, love, go to church, love,
Go to church, love, farewell.

Kneel down, love, kneel down, love,
Kneel down, love, farewell.

Say your prayers, love, say your prayers, love,
Say your prayers, love, farewell.

Stand up, love, stand up, love,
Stand up, love, farewell.

Put the ring on, put the ring on,
Put the ring on, farewell.

Return love, return love,
Return love, farewell.

Give a kiss, love, give a kiss love,
Give a kiss, love, farewell.

Here we go round the jingo-ring,
The jingo-ring, the jingo-ring,
Here we go round the jingo ring,
Around the merry-ma-tansie.

Twice about and then we fall,
Then we fall, then we fall,
Twice about and then we fall,
Around the merry-ma-tansie.

Choose your maidens, one or two,
One or two, one or two,
Choose your maidens, one or two,
Around the merry-ma-tansie.

Sweep the house till the bride comes in,
The bride comes in, the bride comes in,
Sweep the house till the bride comes in,
Around the merry-ma-tansie.

A guinea-gold ring to tell her name,
To tell her name, to tell her name,
A guinea-gold ring to tell her name,
Around the merry-ma-tansie.

Jeannie is her first name,
Her first name, her first name,
Jeannie is her first name,
Around the merry-ma-tansie.

Macdonald is her second name,
Her second name, her second name,
Macdonald is her second name,
Around the merry-ma-tansie.

A bottle of wine to tell his name,
To tell his name, to tell his name,
A bottle of wine to tell his name,
Around the merry-ma-tansie.

Robbie is his first name,
His first name, his first name,
Robbie is his first name,
Around the merry-ma-tansie.

Bruce is his second name,
His second name, his second name,
Bruce is his second name,
Around the merry-ma-tansie.

Uncle John is very sick,
What shall I send him?
A piece of bread, a piece of cake,
A piece of apple dumpling.

Who shall I send it by?
By the governor's daughter.
Take her by the lily-white hand
And lead her across the water.

I knock at the door, I pick up a pin,
And ask *Mrs Buchan*, 'Is *Sheila* within?'
'She's neither within, she's neither without,
She's up in the garret walking about.'

Down she comes as white as milk,
A rose in her bosom as soft as silk;
She off with her glove, and shows me a
     ring,
Tomorrow, tomorrow, the wedding begins.

2. Create a tableau to represent a photo taken at a wedding. At this stage you should try to make the photo as 'neutral' as possible – i.e. do not provide any visual clues beyond marking who is the bride, groom, family, friends, children. The picture should represent the 'public presentation' of the happy event! **10 mins**

3. Organise a presentation of the work done by all the groups. Arrange groups in a circle and present the work so that as we watch one group's wedding photo, the next group plays their game and chant. Rotate around the circle until all groups have shown both their game and photo. What is the effect of linking the games and photos? What themes are suggested? what is the relationship between childhood dreams and the dreams of newly-wed couples? **20 mins**

The devising starts with a consideration of the 'meanings' of love and marriage that we all learn through our culture. The games and the wedding are examples of 'rituals' that are part of this cultural education. This simple sequence focuses on the links between the rituals of childhood and adult life and is presented in a ritual form – a circular, communal performance. The wedding photo – the public face of a marriage – will become a core image that is returned to throughout the devising process. The students will work on scenes leading up to and following this moment. As the work develops the photos will begin to become dramatic – understood in terms of their history and implications for the future.

---

4. Look at the advert which was found in a corner shop. What are the different reasons the woman might have for needing/wanting to sell her wedding dress and rings? Are there any clues about the woman from the details she provides? Together with the other groups make a list of all the reasons that have been suggested so far.

FOR SALE
– <u>Full length white satin wedding dress,</u>
sweetheart neck line, fitted to waist with diamante and pearl embroidery, size 10
£200 ono
– <u>Engagement and wedding rings</u>
set 3 stone engagement ring centre stone emerald + 2 diamonds.
Wishbone style wedding ring
£200 ono
Tel: Jacquie 2098452

---

5. Decide in your group which of the reasons for selling interests you. Now produce a 30-second clip of action that either happens immediately before or after the moment when your wedding photo was taken. The action may be lines spoken between characters which give a different view of the relationship, a significant look passed between characters, or maybe some jostling or pushing to form the wedding group for the photo. Your sequence should include the frozen group

photo immediately after or before the action as appropriate. In this clip you will provide clues that will begin to explain to the rest of the class why the wedding might not work out, or why the wedding couple might, eventually, have to sell/get rid of the dress/rings. Reform the circle to show all the groups' work, find out whether the others spotted the clues that you gave – are you happy with the feedback you got, do you want to change or develop your ideas? **20 mins**

Encourage the groups to be subtle with their clues, i.e. don't over-sign the issue or problem, just hint at it. The students will respond to the 'guessing game' structure. They are being encouraged to translate abstract ideas about the problem into concrete strips of action that represent the problem for an audience. The juxtaposition of off-camera private behaviour and the formality of the photo emphasises the gap between public and private perceptions of the marriage. The devising is led by the creation of 'fragments' like this one which can then be used to make the final montage. Encourage students to avoid creating a strong narrative line for their work at his stage – concentrate on creating the 'actions' while leaving the narrative possibilities open-ended.

6. Think about how the 'problem' on the wedding day might develop. What is the point/moment which drives the woman to sell? How bad does the problem get before she decides she has had enough? Choose the moment when the decision is taken, not the moment when she consciously begins the process of advertising her things. The group shows the moment of 'no turning back' twice: 1) with narration provided by woman, 2) with narration provided by man. The actions that are performed should change to reflect the different perspectives of the narrators. Begin your performance from within the wedding photo. **30–45 mins**

In terms of structure the students are moved straight to the climax. They have to consider how the small clues given previously might develop into a dramatic conclusion. The use of monologues 'distances' the emotional intensity of the scene, (which the students are not yet ready to perform), and draws attention to 'voice' and the potential schism between the protagonists. It also requires the actor to think about the subtle differences of gesture and action needed to faithfully represent the different perspectives on the action.

7. What might the first clues have been that the wedding couple have a problem that will eventually destroy the marriage? How are the seeds of what will happen first sown for an audience? Create the scene which shows the very beginnings of the problem. It might be a scene from early in their relationship – a first meeting perhaps – in which neither character is aware of the problem but the clues are there for an attentive audience. In other words, construct and play the scene so that the 'sub-text' is revealed to the audience but the actors appear not to be aware, or to ignore, that anything is wrong. Again, begin your work from within the wedding photo. **30 mins**

Although this scene is less obviously 'dramatic' than the last it may well produce some powerful performances. The students have just finished working on and performing the climax scene; they are carrying that experience into the playing of this scene. They are doing what actors must do, to perform a moment in the play in the full knowledge of the emotional structure and process of the whole performance. The focus on sub-text creates a tension between what is known to the audience and what is apparently not known by the actors. This scene, which contains the seeds of all that follows, and which is full of inference and subtle signs that will be amplified and clarified by what happens subsequently, would make an ideal opportunity for scripting which could then be passed to another group for rehearsal and performance.

8. Work on two scenes that will be 'cut together' or edited together in the manner of film or TV editing, i.e. rapid cuts from one scene to the next and back, so that the events in one scene are ironically or significantly placed against events in the second scene. Try different possibilities so that what you have is one scene made out of the two in such a way that it is more interesting and revealing than if you had simply played one scene after another.

The two scenes are :
(a) the circumstances in which the ring was bought; involves the man and woman and must include the line 'Are you sure ... about the ring I mean' and a 'gestus' or significant action that is put in for the audience to read. The *gestus* should belong to the scene but also speak louder than the scene, i.e. it should refer to the bigger themes and ideas that lie behind the work so far.
(b) a dialogue between two other characters in which they discuss the forthcoming wedding and which must include the line 'Are you going to say anything, then?' Groups present the 'mix' of their two scenes. **30-45 mins**

The students are creating more 'fragments' for their final montage; exploring each scene so that it stands as a scenic unit in its own right but also, increasingly, each is woven through with references to other moments in the story that is developing – both before and after. The focus on gestus encourages this process and asks students to isolate, select and amplify key gestures and actions that comment on the 'meanings' of the work for the audience. The film editing uses students' existing knowledge of film literacy to think about 'montage': how the fragments they have created can best be assembled.

9. Each group remakes their wedding photo, others are asked to think about the 'distance' between characters and to rearrange them so that the 'distance' is spatially represented. Allow plenty of 'possibles'. Can the distance be named? Will it be the same five years later? The actors should allow themselves to be moved around and listen to how the relationships between characters are being interpreted. When all the suggestions have been made the teacher counts to three and claps. The actors, without discussion, should now move into the

spatial relationship with other characters which they think is the 'true' relationship. **15 mins**

> This exercise, which is apparently quite distanced and analytical, may again produce some powerful effects and realisations. Students' attention should be drawn to the use of space and distance to create (make concrete) and describe abstract meanings.

10. Alternative or multiple closures:

(a) Imagine that the wedding is now well and truly over and that characters from your story are invited as guests on the *Rikki Lake Show*. Use your knowledge of the show (or any similar chat show where people talk about their private lives and problems) to create the show complete with audience, titles, and your very own Rikki Lake compere. Introduce the characters, get them to tell their side/s of the story, bring on secret guests and see whether the characters have 'something special' to say to each other! **20 mins**

(b) Two chairs are placed in the centre of the working space. Props representing the rings and wedding dress are placed on one of the chairs. You will need two volunteers to represent 'the woman who sells the dress' and 'the woman who comes to buy it'. The rest of the group now decide which of the two women they want to speak for and sit behind the appropriate chair: they will be the *collective character* of the woman they choose. The two volunteers cannot speak during the next stage but they can use body language to reinforce, or change, the 'voices' that will speak from behind them. When everyone is ready, carefully improvise the conversation between the two women. What will they say to each other? How might their perceptions of love and marriage be different? What will they want to find out from each other? As the conversation ends, or a sale is made, you might want to repeat the childhood rhymes and chants from the beginning of the structure. **10–15 mins**

> At first sight this must seem a strange juxtaposition between the superficial sentimentality and sensationalism of the 'chat show' and a dramatic confrontation between the 'voices' of innocence and experience. But it is an interesting montage to make. In the first exercise, students are being encouraged to use the post-modern styles of parody and pastiche to comment both on the genre – chat shows – and on the public exploitation of private states of grief. In the second exercise there is a radical difference in the 'feel' and emotional weight as students work on an epic treatment in which the two women socially and historically represent those women who have experienced the 'reality' of love and marriage and those who still believe it can be different. It is the combination of the two, together with the return to the original chants, that forms the 'montage': the assembly of form and content. There should be detailed discussion about the effects of this montage on the students' understanding of the themes and their experience of the drama.

Learning outcomes – What have students learnt from the structure?	Subject objectives – Which objectives have been covered by the structure?
the principles of montage and devising	1.5 Learning to use a variety of processes to devise and perform drama, e.g. improvisation, workshops, rehearsal, scripting, storyboards, characterisation 3.1 Learning and using a critical vocabulary for discussing drama, e.g. gesture, symbol, tension, rhythm and pace, contrast
to use different acting styles associated with Naturalist and post-Naturalist theatre	1.2 Learning how to use and control the elements of drama; particularly the body in space 1.4 Learning to identify and distinguish historical and current genres of drama, e.g. tragedy, comedy, mime, mask, physical, soap opera
to structure and play in the 'dramatic present'	3.1 Learning and using a critical vocabulary for discussing drama, e.g. gesture, symbol, tension, rhythm and pace, contrast
to invite and respond to critical feedback as part of the rehearsal process	3.2 Learning to identify and evaluate the different choices that can be made in drama that lead groups to make different interpretations/representations of the same material 3.3 Learning how to write reviews of drama that accurately refer to what was seen, heard and experienced during the drama
to create a 'scrapbook' of dramatic fragments that can later be used to make a montage or performance piece (alinear devising)	2.2 Learning to work as part of an ensemble – acting and reacting to others 2.3 Learning about the different contributions that actors, audiences, directors, writers, designers and technicians make to a dramatic event 2.4 Learning how to direct the work of writers, actors and designers into a coherent dramatic statement

An A–Z of drama conventions and techniques

This is a collection of frequently used conventions and techniques for structuring drama, simply arranged in alphabetical order. References to these techniques are frequently made in drama teaching texts, policy and curriculum documents. The conventions are not structures in themselves, they are more like the building blocks or palette that is used, alongside others, to create structures. Cookery is a useful analogy here. The list of conventions is like the list of ingredients for a recipe. It is only when the 'ingredients' are combined and subtly blended that they become a satisfying meal (montage)! I have only given here a brief definition of the most popular conventions. For further explanation of the conventions and the conventions approach to structuring see Neelands, J. (ed. Goode, T.) 1990 *Structuring Drama Work*: Cambridge University Press.

Alter-ego	This involves a student other than the one playing the character as an extension of that character. The alter-ego's main function is to express the *feelings* or 'inner speech' of the character. This convention is designed to deepen the collective understanding of how a character might be feeling about a given situation even though the character itself may not be able to express those feelings (text/sub-text). The expression of feeling may be verbal or physical. Very effective when used in conjunction with hot-seating.
Choral speak	A written text is divided up and spoken by group. Text may be dramatic or otherwise. The construction of the choral speak should comment on, or develop, the original text rather than literally follow the line divisions or allocation of lines to single characters. Particularly effective when the choral speak is part of a montage with another convention, e.g. tableau, or mime.
Circular drama	A variation on *small group drama* in which groups are given different scenes involving a central character. The groups prepare the scene and then the *teacher in role* joins each scene as the central character and improvises briefly with each group before moving on. This provides the opportunity to see the different ways in which the central character reacts in a variety of public and private contexts.

Collective character	A character is improvised by a group of students; any one of them can speak as the character. In this way the whole class can be involved in a dialogue, for instance, by half the class taking on one of the characters involved. There doesn't need to be conformity in the responses they make; different attitudes can be given expression so that there is also dialogue between members of the collective character.
Come on down!	Any popular game show format is used if it can either illuminate or make ironic events and characters. Chat-show formats provide an alternative form of *hot-seating*; students should identify and preserve the generic features of the game show in their work.
Conflicting advice	Characters are offered conflicting advice as to what to do about any given situation. This can be done in character by other characters in the drama and by voices in the character's head played by other members of the group. It is possible to develop this convention by allowing the character to engage in conversation with the voices and thus challenge the advice being offered; also the voices themselves may engage in debate with the character listening in.
Conscience alley	At a critical moment in a character's life when a dilemma, problem, or choice must be made, the character walks between two rows of students who may offer advice as the character passes. The advice may be from the students as themselves or from other characters; the advice may include lines or words spoken earlier in the drama.
Defining space	The drama space is carefully marked out into different locations or times. A key space in the drama such as a particular room is reconstructed using available props and furniture.
Documentary	The events of the drama are translated into a documentary format, or characters are established through documentary evidence, cf. *Citizen Kane*.
Flashback	The relationship between the dramatic present and the past is reinforced by showing 'flashback' scenes while the present scene unfolds, or at a crucial moment a character is confronted by images of the past.
Forum theatre	A small group act out a drama for the rest of the group as 'observers'. Both the 'performers' and the 'observers' have the right to stop the drama at any point and make suggestions as to how it might proceed; ask for it to be replayed with changes designed to bring out another point of view or focus; deepen the drama by using any of the other conventions. An important feature is that all the participants, 'performers' and 'observers', take responsibility for the crafting of the drama – the

	responsibility does not lie solely with the 'performers', in fact they are more like puppets responding to their puppeteers.
Gestus	Students present a dramatic sequence which includes a specially loaded action or gesture – something that the audience sees which clearly relates to the broader theme or historical context of the whole performance text as well as belonging to the immediate context the students are creating. A ring that cannot be made to fit; a doll that is carelessly dropped by a negligent parent; a murderer trying to wash her hands.
Gossip circle	The private and public behaviour of characters is commented on in the form of rumours and gossip circulating in the community; as the rumours 'spread' around the circle they become exaggerated and distorted. A useful way of identifying tensions, conflicts and contradictions for further exploration.
Group sculpture	The group, or an individual from the group, models volunteers into a shape, usually of a non-representational nature, which expresses a particular aspect of the theme or issue being addressed. The collective creation of this 'sculpture' will force the group members to bring out their own, individual interpretation of events portrayed in the drama. This is not to be confused with *still photographs* which tend to be literal representations.
Headlines	Statements in the style of newspaper headlines are used to focus the attention on to a particular aspect of the drama. Used with *still photographs* several headlines can be given for the same photograph in order to highlight different points of view and bias.
Hot-seating	Characters are questioned about their values, motives, relationships and actions by other members of the group. This is a very effective rehearsal technique that helps an actor to flesh out and discover new facets of their character through the responses they make to the questions. The questioners may also be in role as witnesses, historians, detectives, etc. There can be added tension if the character is questioned at a moment of stress, or at a turning point in their lives.
Iceberg	A reflective device in which a diagram of an iceberg is drawn. Students have to consider what is text and what is sub-text in a scene and then to note text above the waterline of the iceberg and sub-text beneath the waterline.
Improvisation	A spontaneous acting out of a given situation in which students have to respond to the given circumstances – who, where, when, what. A prepared but unscripted performance or a situation that is prepared by one group of students which is improvised with the teacher-in-role or with volunteers from another group.

Interviews, interrogations	Characters are interviewed by 'reporters' or interrogated by an authority figure in order to question their motives, values, beliefs or to elicit more facts about a given situation.
Letters	Delivered by the teacher/leader to either the whole group or to small sub-groups in order to introduce a new idea, focus or tension to the existing drama. The participants can write them both in and out of character as a means of crystallising thought or reflecting on past action.
Mantle of the expert	The major feature of this convention is that the pupils are in role as characters with specialist knowledge relevant to the situation they find themselves in. In its purest form mantle of the expert requires an approach to teaching and learning that is holistic and therefore cross-curricular; however, I have found that endowing pupils with expertise is in itself extremely powerful, motivating and empowering.
Marking the moment	Allows the participants to reflect on a time within the drama in which strong reactions, emotions or feelings were felt by the individuals within the group. They are reflecting out of character and so the reactions identified are those of the participants themselves, not the characters they were playing. They use any of the other conventions suitable for sharing their moment with the rest of the group.
Meetings	The group get together in order to address some problem or to discuss information within the format of a formal meeting which may be further controlled by the local cultural circumstances of the fiction: power and status of characters, for instance. This is also very useful for the teacher to input information, create atmosphere or inject tension within the fiction rather than stopping the drama in order to do so.
Moment of truth	A technique in which the group must devise a final scene for the drama. They must engage in reflective discussion of the major events and tensions in order to create a sharp focus for the final scene.
Narration	One of the participants tells the story while the others 'act it out', or a series of scenes are linked by narrative which can either simply tell the story or, more importantly, comment on the action from a particular point of view.
Overheard conversations	The group 'listen in' to 'private' conversations between characters in the drama. An interesting and challenging development of this is for the group to agree whether or not the information gained from listening in can be used in the subsequent drama or is it something they must pretend not to know. By enabling the participants to listen into a private conversation the teacher/leader can introduce a new idea, or a

	threat or problem, by creating rumour that will be interpreted in a variety of ways.
Private property	A character is introduced, or constructed, through carefully chosen personal belongings – objects, letters, reports, costume, toys, medals, etc. The intimacy of the information gleaned from these objects may be contrasted with a character who reveals very little about themselves or who presents a contradictory self-image from that suggested by the objects – the private property forms a sub-text to the character's words and actions.
Re-enactments	In order to examine a situation in more detail, a scene or an event that has 'already happened' may be re-enacted. If this is linked into the idea of clarification of fact or confirmation of the source of a rumour it can provide a very powerful focus for checking and confirming the whole group's growing understanding of a given situation.
Reportage	Participants report on a situation in the style of a journalist either from within the drama in character or outside of it out of character. The journalist can work in any media form.
Ritual and ceremony	Students create appropriate rituals and ceremonies that might be celebrated or endured by characters to mark anniversaries, cycles, initiations, belief systems, etc.
Role on the wall	A record of a character is kept in the form of a large outline of a figure in which students might write key lines, phrases, ideas or feelings about the character. The outline is kept and re-edited as students discover more about the character.
Small-group drama	Sub-groups of the whole class work on separate but related interpretations or developments of the major theme.
Soundtracking	Sounds are used to create the atmosphere of the 'place' in which the drama takes place. These can be prerecorded or live and are usually, though not always, created by the participants.
Space between	Students arrange characters so that the space between them represents the distance in their relationship to each other (how near and far apart, who is close to whom). The students can also consider the change in the space over time – will characters draw closer together or further apart? They can also try to name the distance – betrayal, fear, power, etc.
Split-screen	Students plan two or more scenes which occur in different times and places; they then work on cutting backwards and forwards between the two scenes as in film/TV. The edit of the two scenes should be carefully prepared to maximise the links, analogies or irony between the two.
Still photographs/ video pause	The still photo is developed to include the convention of a freeze frame or pause in the action, as if on a video recorder. This allows the group to examine a particular moment in more detail.

Tableau	Participants create a physical image using their own bodies to represent a moment from the drama. Combined with *sound-tracking, thought tracking*, this convention can be used in a variety of different circumstances. Try linking two or more together as a way of developing a narrative sequence or predicting possible outcomes.
Teacher in role	Expressed in its simplest form the teacher/leader takes part in the drama along with the other participants. Teachers often feel extremely reticent, for a variety of reasons, about joining in alongside the children but there is no doubt at all that children respond very positively indeed to their teacher becoming part of the shared act of creating a drama.
Telephone conversations	The listeners hear either one side of the conversation only or both sides depending on the intention of their using the convention. The teacher leader can also use this to add information, develop the narrative or inject tension from within the fiction.
This way – that way	The same scene or events can be played with different narrators; the playing of the scene will be subtly altered according to the narrator's interests and perspective.
Thought tracking	The inner thoughts of a character are revealed either by the person adopting that role or by the others in the group. This is a particularly useful way of slowing down and deepening a drama especially it used in conjunction with *still photographs* or *tableaux*.
Unfinished materials	The group is presented with a piece of writing, drawing, diagram, audio or video tape which is incomplete. Their task is to complete it or solve the problem of why it has not been finished.
Venting	A variation on *thought tracking* in which students can come up and vent the feelings, emotions, confusions, ambiguities in the character's mind at that moment. Several students can vent simultaneously to create a 'dialogue' or to demonstrate different views of the character's state of mind.
Whole-group drama	All of the participants, including, usually, the teacher/leader, are engaged in the same drama at the same time (see also *meetings*).

Bibliography

The rationale/philosophy of drama education

Boal, A. (1994) *The Rainbow of Desire*. Routledge.

Bolton, G. (1984) *Drama as Education (an argument for placing drama at the centre of the curriculum)*. Longman.

Bolton, G. (1992) *New Perspectives on Classroom Drama*. Simon & Schuster.

Hornbrook, D. (1989) *Education and Dramatic Art*. Blackwell.

Hornbrook, D. (1991) *Education in Drama*. Falmer Press.

Johnson L. and O'Neill. D. (eds) (1984) *Dorothy Heathcote: Collected Writings On Education and Drama*. Hutchinson.

McGregor, L. *et al.* (1977) *Learning through Drama*. Heinemann.

O'Neill, C. (1995) *Drama Worlds*. Heinemann US.

O'Toole, J. (1992) *The Process of Drama*. Routledge.

Wagner, B. J. (1972) *Drama as a Learning Medium*. Hutchinson.

Strategies/approachs for teaching drama at KS3

Byron, K. (1982) *Drama in the English Classroom*. Heinemann. A practical exploration of drama's role in deepening responses to reading.

Clarke, J. *et al.* (1997) *Lessons For The Living: Drama in the Transition Years*. Mayfair (Canada). An accessible and useful series of lesson structures and advice on planning and teaching, specially designed for KS3.

Crinson, J. and Leake, L. (Ed.) (1993) *Move Back the Desks*. NATE. An excellent publication giving case studies of drama work in English and guidance in managing drama for non-specialists.

Fleming, M. (1995). *Starting Drama Teaching*. David Fulton Publishers. A crucial introduction for drama teachers which combines some rationale with numerous concrete strategies.

James, R. and Williams, P (1980). *A Guide to Improvisation*. Kemble Press. Gradual, simple and protected steps into the drama teaching situation, offering exercises in verbal and physical drama.

Lewis, R. (1981) *Active Drama*. Heinemann. Offers approaches to teaching the elements of theatre/drama as an introduction to working with scripts.

Morgan, N. and Saxton, J. (1987) *Teaching Drama*. Hutchinson. A comprehensive guide to teaching drama which offers a clear framework of theory and practice. A useful reference for looking at methodology, planning and assessing drama work.

Neelands, J. (1984) *Making Sense of Drama*. Heinemann. Although dated in parts, chapters 3–8 concisely deal with important basic considerations for the approach of the drama teacher, synthesising the work of many educational practitioners.

Neelands, J. (1990) *Structuring Dramawork*. Cambridge University Press. This book defines a range of theatre/drama conventions and principles for structuring and developing drama work and drama-based learning.

Neelands, J. (1992) *Learning through Imagined Experience*. Hodder & Stoughton. A range of strategies which highlight both the value and the possible approaches for introducing learning through drama into the classroom in the context of English in the National Curriculum.

O'Neill, C. (1977) *Drama Guidelines*. Heinemann. Provides a series of straightforward drama structures and ideas for teachers and students who are new to drama. Despite its age it is still a clear and friendly introduction to the drama-in-education tradition.

O'Neill, C. and Lambert, A. (1982) *Drama Structures*. Hutchinson. A trusted reference to key teaching skills and methods, the book also provides a series of well constructed and enjoyable drama structures which can be easily followed or adapted.

Smith, K. (1986) *Stages in Drama*. Foulsham. A real mixture of drama/theatre lesson plans. Intended as a stopgap for non-specialist drama teachers and for cover lessons.

Taylor, K. (1990) *Drama Strategies*. London Drama. Sample lesson plans and basic strategies for drama devised by groups of London teachers.

Taylor, P. (1998) *Redcoats and Patriots: Reflective Practice in Drama and Social Studies*. Heinemann (USA). Considers the role of drama in social studies through the eyes of a teacher who is introducing these approaches in his classroom.

Beyond KS3

Boagey, E. (1986) *Starting Drama*. Unwin Hyman. A series of ideas for lessons using theatre history and the elements of staging plays as material.

Cooper, S. and Mackey, S. (1995). *Theatre Studies: An Approach for Advanced Level*. A detailed student text that covers the AEB syllabus requirements and is also a useful general guide to theatre studies.

Fleming, M. (1997) *The Art of Drama Teaching*. David Fulton Publishers. Explores a variety of theatre conventions through extracts from dramatic literature and exercises.

Kempe, A. (1988). *Drama Sampler: An Approach to Work on Scripts for Exam Work*. Blackwell. Includes a range of extracts and imaginative ways of working with them.

Kempe, A. *The GCSE Drama Coursebook*. Blackwell. Designed as a student textbook by an author who takes a particular interest in working with scripts. Many of the ideas and extracts are now appropriate to KS3.

Marson, P. *et al.* (1990). *Drama 14–16 – A Book of Projects and Resources*. Stanley Thornes. Through a range of drama projects offers strategies and devices for creating dramas in the classroom.

O'Toole, J. and Haseman, B. (1987). *Dramawise*. Heinemann. One of the first books to look at the teaching of the formal elements of drama within contexts that are relevant and meaningful for students. An excellent bridge between 'drama' and 'theatre' which includes projects, lesson plans and exercises for students

Teaching Shakespeare

Ackroyd, J. *et al.* (1998) *Key Shakespeare Book 1*. Hodder.

Gilmour, M. (1997) *Shakespeare in Secondary Schools*. Cassell.

Gilmour, M. (ed.) (1997) *Shakespeare for All in the Primary School*. Cassell.

Leach, S. (1992) *Shakespeare in the Classroom*. O.U. Press.

O'Brien, V. (1982) *Teaching Shakespeare*. Edward Arnold.

Pinder, B. (1992) *Shakespeare: An Active Approach*. Unwin Hyman.

I.T. and Drama

Neelands, J. (1993) *Discovering the Human Dimension: I.T. and Drama*. NATE.

Media

Bazalgette, C. (1991) *Media Education*. Hodder and Stoughton.

Branston, G. (1996) *The Media Handbook*. Routledge.

Buckingham, D. *et al.* (1995) *Making Media: Learning from Media Production*. NATE.

Grahame, J. (1991) *The English Curriculum: Media Years 7–9*. NATE English and Media Centre.

Hart, A. (1991) *Understanding the Media*. Routledge.

Lusted, D. (1991) *The Media Studies Book – A Guide for Teachers*. Routledge.

Philo, G. (1990) *Seeing and Believing –The Influence of Television*. Routledge.

Drama games

Brandes, D. and Phillips, H. (1978) *Gamesters' Handbook (140 Games for Teachers and Group Leaders)*. Hutchinson.

Brandes, D. (1982) *Gamesters' Handbook Two*. Hutchinson.

Scher, A and Verrall, C. (1975) *100+ Ideas for Drama*. Heinemann.

Scher, A. and Verrall, C. (1975) *Another 100+ Ideas for Drama*. Heinemann.

Theatre/actor training

Barker, C. (1977) *Theatre Games*. Methuen.

Boal, A. (1979) *Games for Actors and Non-Actors*. Routledge.

Hodgson, J. and Richards, E. (1966) *Improvisation*. Eyre Methuen.

Johnstone, K. (1979) *Impro*. Methuen.

Miles-Brown, J. (1985) *Acting: A Drama Studio Source Book*. Peter Owen.

Modern theatre texts and performance theory

Artaud, A. (1970) *The Theatre and its Double*. Calder & Boyars.

Aston, E. and Savona, G. (1992) *Theatre as Sign System*. Routledge.

Barba, E. & Savarese, N. (1991) *A Dictionary of Theatre Anthropology: The Secret Art of the Performer*. Routledge.

Beckerman, B. 1990) *Theatrical Presentation*. Routledge.

Boal, A. (1979) *Theatre of the Oppressed*. Pluto Press.

Braun, E. (1982) *The Director and the Stage: From Naturalism to Grotowski*. Methuen.

Brook, P. (1968) *The Empty Space*. Penguin.

Counsell, C. (1996) *Signs of Performance: A History of Twentieth Century Theatre*. Routledge.

Drain, R. (1995) *Twentieth Century Theatre: A Reader*. Routledge.

Esslin, M. (1987) *The Field of Drama*. Methuen.

Fuegi, J. (1987) *Bertolt Brecht – Chaos according to Plan*. Cambridge University Press.

Grotowski, J. (1969) *Towards A Poor Theatre*. Methuen.

Magarshack, D. *Stanislavski: A Life*. Methuen.

Schechner, R. (1988) *Performance Theory*. University Paperbacks.

Styan, J. L. (1978) *Modern Drama in Theory and Practice: Part 1 – Naturalism and Realism*. Cambridge University Press.

Styan, J. L. (1978) *Modern Drama in Theory and Practice: Part 2 – Symbolism, Surrealism and the Absurd*. Cambridge University Press.

Styan, J. L. *Modern Drama in Theory and Practice: Part 3 – Expressionism and Epic Theatre* Cambridge University Press.

Willet, J. (ed.) (1964) *Brecht on Theatre*. Methuen.

Williams, R. (1968) *Drama from Ibsen to Brecht*. Methuen.